An Introduction to
WITTGENSTEIN'S
Philosophy of Religion

An Introduction to
WITTGENSTEIN'S
Philosophy of Religion

Brian R. Clack

Edinburgh University Press

For
Jonathan Herapath
and
Helen O'Sullivan

Copyright for the Wittgenstein extracts is held by the publishers who details appear on page xi and xii.

The author gratefully acknowledges these sources.

© Brian R. Clack, 1999

Transferred to digital print 2006

Edinburgh University Press,
22 George Square,
Edinburgh

Typeset in Ehrhardt
by Hewer Text Ltd, Edinburgh

A CIP record for this book is available from the British Library

ISBN-10 0 7486 0939 3
ISBN-13 9 7807 4860 939 0

The right of Brian R. Clack
to be identified as author of this work
has been asserted in accordance with
the Copyright, Designs and Patents Act 1988.

I could imagine somebody might admire not only real trees, but also the shadows or reflections that they cast, taking them too for trees. But once he has told himself that these are not really trees after all and has come to be puzzled at what they are, or at how they are related to trees, his admiration will have suffered a rupture that will need healing.

Ludwig Wittgenstein, 1947

CONTENTS

PREFACE

Thirty years ago, Donald Hudson's *Ludwig Wittgenstein: The Bearing of his Philosophy upon Religious Belief* was published. It was the first introduction to Wittgenstein's thought on religion and was characterised by brevity, admirable clarity and simplicity of expression. Here was a book intended to make the thought of a notoriously difficult philosopher accessible to students and to those outside of academia. Since that book's publication more of Wittgenstein's writings have appeared, and, having taught courses on Wittgenstein over a number of years, I became aware of the need for a similarly short introduction which could give students an overview of the main elements of his thinking on religion. While there are other excellent texts on this subject (most significantly, those of Cyril Barrett and Fergus Kerr), there is no book which quite fills the gap left by the superannuation of Hudson's text. Hence this book, which will, I hope, serve to illustrate to students of theology, philosophy and religious studies, as well as to the interested lay-reader, the nature and abiding significance of Wittgenstein's extraordinary thoughts on religious belief and practice.

The first chapter serves as an introduction to Wittgenstein's life and to the main features of his early and later philosophy, as elaborated in his two great works, *Tractatus Logico-Philosophicus* and *Philosophical Investigations*. I then consider Wittgenstein's earliest thoughts on the nature of religion and 'the mystical', before moving into an exposition of his mature writings on such matters as magic, the Last Judgement and God. Chapter 4 considers the philosophy of religion offered by some of Wittgenstein's followers (including Norman Malcolm and D. Z. Phillips), and here the characteristically Wittgensteinian talk of language-games and its application to such matters as the miraculous and immortality is assessed. A final chapter returns to Wittgenstein, addressing his relation both to mainstream philosophy of religion and to recent radical theology. I also reflect on whether his account of religion is compatible with continued belief.

The writing of this book would have proved impossible without the assistance of many people. I would first like to thank Jane Feore at Edinburgh University Press for her initial interest in the project, continuous encouragement, and unceasing patience with a sluggish author. My family have, once again, been a great source of support: thanks go to my father Alan Clack, my sister Beverley Clack, and to my mother Ann Clack, whose endurance I have once again pushed to the extreme. I also owe an enormous debt of gratitude to Adam Clayton, who has for many years now been a great source of strength and whose influence has been immeasurable. And I can only hint at what I owe to Celia Stringer, who has given me more love than I deserve and who makes every moment of my life a joy. Celia's reflections on early drafts of this book were invaluable. As this book is the result of years of teaching courses on Wittgenstein, it is only right that I should extend the final words of thanks to all those students (at Heythrop College, Westminster College, St. Catherine's College, and St. Clare's) who contributed so heartily to my classes. Of these students, special mention must be made of Jonathan Herapath and Helen O'Sullivan, who attended my seminars for three long years and whose friendship I now treasure. To them I dedicate this book.

B. R. C.
Oxford, August 1998

Note
'He' and 'she', 'his' and 'hers', are used interchangeably in this book, so in appropriate contexts import the common gender.

ABBREVIATIONS

The following abbreviations are used to refer to works by Wittgenstein:

BB   *The Blue and Brown Books*, Oxford: Basil Blackwell, 1958.

BT   'Philosophy: Sections 86–93 of the so-called "Big Typescript" ', ed. Heikki Nyman, trans. C. G. Luckhardt and M. A. E. Aue, in *Ludwig Wittgenstein: Philosophical Occasions 1912–1951*, ed. James Klagge and Alfred Nordmann, Indianapolis: Hackett, 1993, pp. 161–99.

CE   'Cause and Effect: Intuitive Awareness', ed. Rush Rhees, trans. Peter Winch, *Philosophia*, vol. 6, nos. 3–4, September-December 1976, pp. 409–25.

CV   *Culture and Value*, ed. G. H. von Wright in collaboration with Heikki Nyman, trans. Peter Winch, Oxford: Basil Blackwell, 1980.

L   *Letters to Russell, Keynes and Moore*, ed. G. H. von Wright, Oxford: Basil Blackwell, 1974.

LC   *Lectures and Conversations on Aesthetics, Psychology and Religious Belief*, ed. C. Barrett, Oxford: Basil Blackwell, 1966.

LE   'A Lecture on Ethics', *Philosophical Review*, vol. 74 no. 1, January 1965, pp. 3–12.

LF   'Letters to Ludwig von Ficker', ed. Allan Janik, trans. Bruce Gillette, in *Wittgenstein: Sources and Perspectives*, ed. C. G. Luckhardt, Hassocks: Harvester Press, 1979, pp. 82–98.

LFM   *Wittgenstein's Lectures on the Foundations of Mathematics*, ed. Cora Diamond, Chicago: University of Chicago Press, 1989.

NB   *Notebooks 1914–1916*, ed. G. H. von Wright and G. E. M. Anscombe, trans. G. E. M. Anscombe, Oxford: Basil Blackwell, 1961.

OC   *On Certainty*, ed. G. E. M. Anscombe and G. H. von Wright, trans. Denis Paul and G. E. M. Anscombe, Oxford: Basil Blackwell, 1969.

PI   *Philosophical Investigations*, ed. G. E. M. Anscombe and Rush
        Rhees, trans. G. E. M. Anscombe, Oxford: Basil Blackwell,
        1953.
PR   *Philosophical Remarks*, ed. Rush Rhees, trans. Raymond Har-
        greaves and Roger White, Oxford: Basil Blackwell, 1975.
RFGB   *Remarks on Frazer's Golden Bough*, ed. Rush Rhees, trans. A. C.
        Miles and Rush Rhees, Retford: Brynmill Press, 1979.
RFM   *Remarks on the Foundations of Mathematics*, ed. G. H. von
        Wright, R. Rhees, G. E. M. Anscombe, trans. G. E. M.
        Anscombe, Oxford: Basil Blackwell, 1956.
TLP   *Tractatus Logico-Philosophicus*, trans. D. F. Pears and B. F.
        McGuinness, London: Routledge and Kegan Paul, 1961.
VC   *Ludwig Wittgenstein and the Vienna Circle: Conversations Re-
        corded by Friedrich Waismann*, ed. Brian McGuinness, trans.
        Joachim Schulte and Brian McGuinness, New York: Barnes and
        Noble, 1979.
WLA   *Wittgenstein's Lectures, Cambridge 1932–1935*, ed. Alice Am-
        brose, Oxford: Basil Blackwell, 1979.
WLL   *Wittgenstein's Lectures, Cambridge 1930–1932*, ed. Desmond
        Lee, Oxford: Basil Blackwell, 1980.
Z   *Zettel*, ed. G. E. M. Anscombe and G. H. von Wright, trans. G.
        E. M. Anscombe, Oxford: Basil Blackwell, 1981.

LUDWIG WITTGENSTEIN: HIS LIFE AND PHILOSOPHIES

By the time of his death in 1951, Ludwig Wittgenstein had launched philosophy in two divergent directions. The only book he published in his lifetime, the *Tractatus Logico-Philosophicus*, had pointed the way towards the rabidly atheistic tendencies of the Vienna Circle, while his later work, in its patient attention to the subtleties of language, spawned what became known as 'linguistic philosophy'. Neither of these particular directions seems promising if what one wants is an illumination of religion: the former perspective will tell us that religious language is by its very nature nonsensical, while Wittgenstein's later enterprise rejects speculation in favour of the 'quiet weighing of linguistic facts' (Z §447), resulting only in 'a synopsis of trivialities'.[1] Indeed, when one is first exposed to Wittgenstein's major works, it may be felt that we have here a cold and technical philosophy, ill-suited to the life of the spirit. And yet there is something about Wittgenstein's character and his mode of living which seems somewhat out of step with that coolness. In Wittgenstein we encounter a man who desired to become a monk; a man who spurned money and whose ascetic and reclusive lifestyle led some to view him as a modern saint; a man who inspired blind devotion in his 'disciples'; a man who wrote of one of his books that it was 'written to the glory of God' (PR 7). That haunting personality, coupled with the posthumous discovery of some extraordinary writings on religious belief and practice, has entailed that within fifty years of his death Wittgenstein's impact on both the philosophy of religion and theology has been enormous. What is it about this man and his work that could have yielded such a result? This book seeks an answer to that question.

Ludwig Josef Johann Wittgenstein was born in Vienna on 26 April 1889. He was the son of Karl Wittgenstein, an enormously rich steel magnate and prominent patron of the arts. At the very centre of Viennese cultural life, the comings and goings at the Wittgenstein household must have been remarkable to behold: Brahms was a frequent visitor, and the great Secessionist artist Gustav Klimt produced a portrait of Gretl, one of

Ludwig's sisters. There were two other sisters – Hermine and Helene – and four brothers, of whom three – Hans, Kurt and Rudolf – were to commit suicide. The fourth brother, the able pianist Paul, lost an arm in the First World War, and it was for him that Ravel composed his Concerto for the Left Hand. Ludwig was the youngest of the eight children, and though the Wittgenstein family was of Jewish descent, he was baptised in the Catholic Church, the religion of his mother.

The young Ludwig displayed great talents, though not initially in the arena of philosophy. His major interest was in technology and he succeeded in building, at the age of ten, a working sewing-machine. This technical aptitude characterised Wittgenstein's later education. He attended the Realschule in Linz, where he was a contemporary of Adolf Hitler. By all accounts, Wittgenstein's three years at Linz were miserable. He did not adjust well from the cultured atmosphere of his Viennese home to the loutish behaviour of the working-class pupils he encountered at the Realschule. They were unlike any people he had met before, and he was disgusted by them: they were '*Mist*' ('Muck'). The feeling of suspicion was mutual: to his fellow pupils Wittgenstein seemed 'like a being from another world'.[2] In the person of Wittgenstein they encountered an aloof and somewhat frail boy, one who was afflicted with a stammer, and who was the son of one of the richest men in Austria. It was inevitable that Ludwig would not be popular: in his notebooks he speaks of his 'suffering in class'.[3] It must have been with great relief that Wittgenstein in 1906 left the taunts of the Realschule, although he described the subsequent six years of his life as ones of constant unhappiness. He left Linz for Berlin, attending the Technische Hochschule in Charlottenburg, where he studied mechanical engineering, developing there an interest in aeronautics, an interest which brought him, in 1908, to Manchester University. The problems Wittgenstein encountered in engineering led his thoughts towards logic and the foundations of mathematics. In 1911 he travelled to Jena to speak with the great logician Gottlob Frege, who advised Wittgenstein to study at Cambridge under Bertrand Russell.

Thus it was that he entered Trinity College, where Russell supervised his early work on the problems of logic. Wittgenstein made an enormous impact upon Russell, who produced some memorable descriptions of his character at this time. For Russell, Wittgenstein constituted 'the most perfect example I have ever known of genius as traditionally conceived, passionate, profound, intense, and dominating':

> His disposition is that of an artist, intuitive and moody. He says every morning he begins his work with hope, and every evening he ends in despair.[4]

The despair was real. On numerous occasions Wittgenstein threatened suicide, a threat which, given the fate of his brothers, cannot be seen as mere posturing. And it was this intensity of character which was applied to logical and philosophical problems. He made such rapid progress that Russell could say to an astonished Hermine Wittgenstein, 'We expect the next big step in philosophy to be taken by your brother.'[5] Wittgenstein was then only twenty-three years old.

A desire for solitude and isolation led Wittgenstein to Norway, where he intended to pursue his researches away from what he saw as the stifling and superficial atmosphere in Cambridge. Russell tried to dissuade him:

> I said it would be dark, & he said he hated daylight. I said it would be lonely, & he said he prostituted his mind talking to intelligent people. I said he was mad & he said God preserve him from sanity. (God certainly will.)[6]

In 1913, then, rejecting Russell's advice, Wittgenstein temporarily departed from England, lodging in a village called Skjolden, before building himself a small log cabin on the side of the Sogne fjord. Hermine tells us that while in Norway Wittgenstein lived 'in a heightened state of intellectual intensity which verged on the pathological'.[7] Wittgenstein's letters from this period certainly testify to this: he speaks of his depression, of his mental torment, of his wish either to become more intelligent or to die (L 45–7). In short, 'I often think I am going mad' (L 44).

War broke out in 1914 and Wittgenstein welcomed the opportunities it provided for him, principally the opportunity of facing death. It seemed to him that here was the possibility for both intellectual advance and moral betterment:

> Perhaps the nearness of death will bring light into life. God enlighten me.

> Now I should have the chance to be a decent human being, for I'm standing eye to eye with death.[8]

Hence, despite a double hernia, which could have excused him from military service, Wittgenstein volunteered for the Austrian army and, indeed, sought a dangerous posting. As a soldier he suffered once again the same cruelties he had experienced at Linz: his fellow soldiers on the eastern front were 'a band of pigs', 'malicious and heartless people' in whom it was 'almost impossible to find a trace of humanity'.[9] And yet the experience of war proved productive: by the time of his capture and incarceration as a prisoner of war in Cassino, Wittgenstein had completed the book which he said solved all the problems of philosophy, the *Tractatus Logico-Philosophicus*.[10]

The *Tractatus* addresses a number of important philosophical and logical questions, but its most lasting legacy is Wittgenstein's conception of the nature and function of language. The problem with which Wittgenstein is concerned is what it takes for language to be meaningful, to have sense and not to be nonsense. More broadly, Wittgenstein is concerned with the relation of language to the world. How do the words which we speak, think or write relate to the world in which we find ourselves? How does language connect with the world? Wittgenstein's solution to this problem has become known as *the picture theory of meaning*. In essence, this states that language is related to the world in that it 'pictures' (possible or actual) factual situations in the world, and is meaningful only insofar as it fulfils this function.

Some illumination on this can be gained when we consider how it was that Wittgenstein came to this conclusion. During the war, Wittgenstein chanced upon a magazine article which recounted the events in a court case in Paris. The case was concerned with a road accident which had occurred and, to make the circumstances of the accident perfectly plain, a model of the accident had been constructed for the benefit of the judge and jurors. The model was a small-scale reconstruction of the accident: model cars and small model people were used in place of the actual cars and actual people involved in the accident. It came to Wittgenstein with the force of a revelation that language must fulfil the same function with regard to the world that this court-room model did with regard to the traffic accident. In other words, language must be a model of, or must picture, the world. Hence, we read in his notebook the following remark, entered on 29 September 1914:

> In the proposition a world is as it were put together experimentally. (As when in the law-court in Paris a motor-car accident is represented by means of dolls, etc.). (NB 7)

This conception of language and its fundamentally pictorial function chimes with Wittgenstein's belief that *hieroglyphics* was the form of language which most clearly showed its essential nature. 'In order to understand the essential nature of a proposition, we should consider hieroglyphic script, which depicts the facts that it describes' (TLP 4.016).[11] So the idea that came to Wittgenstein was, first, that a proposition, a statement, pictured a fact and, second, that 'each word is a representation of what it stands for' (NB 7). In other words, each word is a representation of an object, the name of some thing. Having made, in the *Notebooks*, the connection between language and hieroglyphics, Wittgenstein proceeds to draw a picture of two figures:

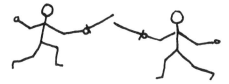

About this he writes:

> If the right-hand figure in this picture represents the man A, and the left-hand one stands for the man B, then the whole might assert, e.g.: 'A is fencing with B'. The proposition in picture-writing can be true and false. It has a sense independent of its truth or falsehood. It must be possible to demonstrate everything essential by considering this case. (NB 7)

Note that Wittgenstein says that 'everything essential' about language can be ascertained by consideration of the fencing hieroglyph. Here the ideas are: first, that the picture asserts something; second, that the assertion could be false (A and B might not be fencing); and third, that regardless of whether the assertion is true or false, the picture has *sense*, so that sense is independent of truth. Consider the sentence 'Buckingham Palace is in London': this sentence asserts something, and what it asserts is correct because Buckingham Place is indeed situated in London. But even if Buckingham Palace was *not* in London (if, say, it was instead in Newcastle) the statement would still have sense, since it would picture a possible (though, as it happens, not an actual) state of affairs.

It is this fundamental idea about the pictorial nature of language that is fully worked out in the *Tractatus*. The following block of comments forcefully express the picture conception:

4.01   A proposition is a picture of reality.
        A proposition is a model of reality as we imagine it.
4.011   At first sight a proposition – one set out on the printed page, for
        example – does not seem to be a picture of the reality with which it is
        concerned. But neither do written notes seem at first sight to be a
        picture of a piece of music, nor our phonetic notation (the alphabet) to
        be a picture of our speech.
        And yet these sign-languages prove to be pictures . . . of what they
        represent.
4.021   A proposition is a picture of reality: for if I understand a proposition, I
        know the situation that it represents.
4.024   To understand a proposition means to know what is the case if it is true.

Understanding language thus means being able to imagine the situation which a particular proposition pictures. If someone tells us that it is raining outside, we will piece together in our mind a picture (e.g.) of water falling from the sky, of the street being wet, of people sheltering under umbrellas.

Of course, what we have been told may not be correct, and 'in order to tell whether a picture is true or false we must compare it with reality' (TLP 2.223). If on going outside we find the sun shining, a dry pavement and a cloudless sky, we will conclude that 'it is raining outside' is a false statement (though not, of course, a senseless one).

So the purpose of language is to describe situations as we find them in the world, to depict and to report *facts*. To offer a proposition is to offer an account of how things are in the world. Indeed, when Wittgenstein comes to define the essence of a proposition, he says, 'The general form of a proposition is: This is how things stand' (TLP 4.5). It is as though every time one spoke, that formula were placed at the beginning of one's remark, so that one might say: 'This is how things stand: It is raining'; 'This is how things stand: Wittgenstein published one book in his lifetime'; and so on.

Wittgenstein's thesis is not, however, simply a thesis about language. It is also a thesis about the world, for in order for language adequately to depict it, the world must be the kind of thing that is capable of being so pictured. And it is indeed Wittgenstein's contention that language and the world share a common structure which makes possible this pictorial relationship. In order to show this, the *Tractatus* offers a classic analysis of the nature of the world. This analysis begins with the very first sentence of the book:

The world is all that is the case. (TLP 1)

This provides us with a definition of the world: it is 'all that is the case'. For Wittgenstein, a *fact* is defined as 'what is the case' and hence 'the world is the totality of facts' (TLP 1.1). He is careful to say that the world does not comprise the totality of 'things', but nevertheless it is these 'things' which are the ultimate building blocks of the world.[12] The reason why a fact cannot be such a building block is because a fact is something *complex*, something which is built out of simpler things. And Wittgenstein's analysis, both of the world and of language, ultimately reaches its bedrock at something totally indivisible, something, as it were, *atomic*. This is why the theory of the *Tractatus* is often labelled *logical atomism*. This requires some clarification.

Atomism is an ancient and distinguished philosophy associated predominantly with the early Greek philosophers Leucippus, Democritus and Epicurus. It attempts to combine our experience of a changeable world with the compelling feeling that underlying this change there must be something unchangeable. The apparent contradiction between change and stasis is resolved in atomism by acknowledging change but contending that change only comes about via the varying combinations and configurations of atoms which are themselves unchanging, indivisible and, indeed, eternal. Existing (or just possible) situations are the result, then, of combinations of atoms, which themselves constitute the primary substance of the world. Though rejected by Plato and Aristotle, atomism was revived by the empiricist philosophers of the seventeenth century, principally Pierre Gassendi and John Locke. The corpuscular theory of these philosophers contended that things are to be explained in terms of their atomic or *corpuscular* constitution, in terms, that is, of the simple atoms out of which they are built. This corpuscular theory forms the basis of modern science. The *Tractatus*, also, advances a form of this ancient philosophy.

The world, says Wittgenstein, consists of facts. But facts are complex entities and can thus be broken down into their constituent parts. To this end, thesis 2 of the *Tractatus* states: 'What is the case – a fact – is the existence of states of affairs' (TLP 2). Similarly, however, a state of affairs is a complex entity and can also be broken down into *its* constituents. Thus, we find Wittgenstein writing, 'A state of affairs (a state of things) is a combination of objects (things)' (TLP 2.01). So Wittgenstein's analysis of the world reveals a tripartite hierarchy of complexity, starting from *facts*, compounded out of *states of affairs* which are themselves made up of 'a combination of objects'. Wittgenstein's atomism manifests itself not just in the dissection of complex entities into smaller ones, but also in his analysis of those small objects themselves. Hence:

2.02   Objects are simple.
2.021   Objects make up the substance of the world. This is why they cannot be composite.
2.0271   Objects are what is unalterable and subsistent; their configuration is what is changing and unstable.

The metaphysical vision of the *Tractatus* is thus that the world consists of innumerable indivisible atoms (or simple objects) which come together to form states of affairs and facts, and then disperse to create new situations. This picture accounts for change while also describing the basic elements of matter.

What is of crucial importance here is the way in which this structure of the world, as conceived by Wittgenstein, enables language to fulfil its pictorial function. Wittgenstein's fundamental contention is that a perfect isomorphism (or one-to-one correlation) exists between the world and language; that language and the world have a shared *logical form*; that their structures *mirror* one another. Just as the world comprises the decreasingly complex trinity of *facts, states of affairs,* and *objects,* so language is shown to have a corresponding threefold structure.

Regarding language, then, we have, first of all, *propositions,* such as 'the cat sat on the mat'. Such propositions serve to depict facts. Thus it is that the third and most complex aspect of the world is mirrored by the third and most complex aspect of language, the proposition. And when Wittgenstein comes to define the nature of a proposition he does this by saying, 'A proposition is a truth-function of elementary propositions' (TLP 5). Just, then, as a fact is composed out of states of affairs, so propositions are composed out of smaller linguistic components called 'elementary propositions', which are depictions of states of affairs. But, of course, it does not stop here: elementary propositions are complex and can be further broken down. When fully analysed, elementary propositions can be shown to be concatenations of what Wittgenstein calls 'names' or 'simple signs'. Such simple signs refer to those simple atomic objects which make up the structure of the world. Hence:

3.203   A name means an object. The object is its meaning.
3.22   In a proposition a name is the representative of an object.

The meaning of a word is the object to which it refers. And the meaning of a proposition is the fact it depicts.

This conception aims to solve the problem of how language manages to speak about the world, the problem of how words relate to things and to facts. Wittgenstein's solution is to maintain that in language, *names* take the place of the *objects* found in the world. To put it another way, names *go proxy* for objects. If I wish to vote in an election, but am unable on that day to reach a polling station, a person chosen by me may vote in my place according to my wishes. Such a procedure is called 'voting by proxy'. In similar fashion, then, the propositions, elementary propositions, and names of *language* go proxy for the corresponding facts, states of affairs, and objects to be found in the *world.* This proxy relation makes the process of communication less cumbersome than it would be were we to have to point to objects every time we wished to make reference to them: instead of hunting around for a cat whenever we wished to refer to such a creature, we simply use the word 'cat' in its place. Schematically presented, the *Tractatus* thus presents us with the following conception of the isomorphic structures of world and language:

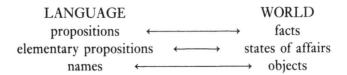

When thinking about Wittgenstein's use of the terms 'name' and 'object', it is important to bear in mind that what he means by these are not what we would normally think of as names and objects. For instance, if we consider the proposition 'the cat sat on the mat', we are tempted to think that the word 'cat' is here a name referring to an object (a cat). But that is *not* what Wittgenstein means, because a cat is obviously something divisible: it can be cut up into pieces or analysed into its constituent atoms and molecules. If we then request from Wittgenstein an example of a real name or object, he seems curiously unable to help us. Wittgenstein never once produced an example of what he meant by each of these things, though he did rack his brains over the issue, putting the following entry into his wartime notebook:

> It does not go against our feeling, that *we* cannot analyse PROPOSITIONS so far as to mention the elements by name; no, we feel that the WORLD must consist of elements. (NB 62)

It may seem quite bizarre that an essential doctrine of the *Tractatus* should be based upon nothing more than an intuition, but Wittgenstein's feeling at this time was that it was not *his* task – as a logician – to identify the objects which make up the world. Such an investigation could only be undertaken by an empirical scientist. Wittgenstein later regarded this view as absurd and indeed came, as we shall see, wholeheartedly to reject the atomistic doctrine of simple objects.

Regardless of the minutiae of atomic propositions and objects, however, the *Tractatus* does offer a clear and plausible account of the nature and function of language. This function is to depict facts, and to understand a statement is to understand the fact that it depicts, to know what the world would look like if that statement were true. Though this may seem to fit in well with much of our everyday experience of language, the consequences of the Tractarian conception are actually rather extreme. Wittgenstein is contending that language has sense only insofar as it serves to picture possible facts. In effect, this means that meaningful language is entirely restricted to empirical or scientific discourse. In Wittgenstein's own words, 'The totality of true propositions is the whole of natural science' (TLP 4.11). Having digested this point, one is then struck by the subsequent remark: 'Philosophy is not one of the natural sciences' (TLP 4.111). If, then, meaningful language is restricted to the empirical sciences, the language of philosophy must therefore be devoid of meaning. And this is indeed the conclusion drawn. Hence Wittgenstein's famous words in the closing sections of the *Tractatus*:

> 6.54   My propositions serve as elucidations in the following way: anyone who understands me eventually recognizes them as nonsensical, when he has used them – as steps – to climb up beyond them. (He must, so to speak, throw away the ladder after he has climbed up it.)

The *Tractatus*, then, enables the reader to gain a clear view of the world and of language, but because it is written in the language of philosophy it must be, strictly speaking, nonsensical. Philosophy is nonsensical for Wittgenstein for many reasons, but principally because it extends beyond the bounds of language. At 5.6 Wittgenstein stresses that the limits of language are the limits of the world. Philosophy, however, typically treats not of the factual situations which we find in the empirical world, but of what is often said to be 'beyond the world' or 'beyond experience'. Such things have no place within the schema of the *Tractatus*, for language has sense only insofar as it pictures the world. An attempt to talk about what is 'beyond the world' is thus quite hopeless. If someone attempted to do this – attempted, that is, to engage in metaphysics – we would have 'to demonstrate to him that he had failed to give a meaning to certain signs in his propositions' (TLP 6.53), that he failed adequately to connect his language to the world.

Within this scientifically-biased picture, it is not just the language characteristic of philosophy that is negated. The language of ethics and of aesthetics is also dismissed: 'it is impossible for there to be propositions of ethics' (TLP 6.42). This injunction arises in part from a perceived discrepancy between, on the one hand, such statements as 'Mr X stole a loaf of bread from the supermarket' and 'Leonardo da Vinci painted the Mona Lisa', and, on the other, the value judgements 'Stealing is wrong' and 'The Mona Lisa is a beautiful painting.' While the former set of statements fulfils the pictorial requirement of meaning, the latter depict nothing and are therefore without sense. It should go without saying that theological discourse – the language of religion – also fails to satisfy the exacting demands of meaningfulness. Concerning these deviations from empirical, factual discourse there is only one possibility:

> 7   What we cannot speak about we must pass over in silence.[13]

By thus demarcating the bounds of sense, Wittgenstein felt that he had both fully articulated the function of language and solved the problems with which philosophy had been wrestling for centuries. Of course, these problems had not so much been solved as shown to be 'nonsensical' since they violated the criteria of meaning required for significance (TLP 4.003). Having achieved this task, Wittgenstein abandoned philosophy and during the 1920s he pursued other activities. Until 1926 he taught in elementary schools in peasant regions of Austria. Though this suited his desire to live well away from the sophistication of 'intelligent people', Wittgenstein once again encountered hostility from 'inhuman beings'[14] (this time the parents of those he taught), who viewed him with much suspicion. Accused of brutality towards his pupils, Wittgenstein eventually returned to Vienna, working as a gardener for the monks at Hüsseldorf and living for three months in the tool-shed of the garden. Gardening proved extremely therapeutic for Wittgenstein, but it was his next non-philosophical project that was of lasting significance.

Wittgenstein's sister Gretl had asked a family friend, the architect Paul Engelmann, to design and construct a house for her in Vienna. In 1926, she and Engelmann invited Wittgenstein to assist in the project, which quickly became his own. Wittgenstein undertook the design of the house with passion, meticulously monitoring every detail, down to the exact size and shape of window-locks and radiators. The Kundmanngasse house is possessed of a stark beauty, all the more remarkable because of the lack of ornamentation, a feature which makes the building hugely reminiscent of the architecture of Adolf Loos. Hermine Wittgenstein's description of the building as 'house embodied logic' very much captures its spirit, a spirit which chimes with the character of his philosophical work. Wittgenstein, moreover, located affinities between the philosophical and the architectural task: 'Working in philosophy – like work in architecture in many respects – is really more a working on oneself . . . On one's way of seeing things' (CV 16).

In 1929 Wittgenstein returned to Cambridge. What it was that provoked this re-embracing of philosophy is not entirely clear. Perhaps it was his encounter with the philosophers of the Vienna Circle during the late 1920s. Or it may have been the interest aroused in him by L. E. J. Brouwer's philosophy of mathematics. More wildly perhaps, it has even been suggested that Wittgenstein returned to Cambridge to act as a Soviet spy-recruiter.[15] What does appear to be the case is that Wittgenstein came to see grave flaws in his earlier theories and sought to resolve those problems. A charming, though possibly apocryphal story illustrates how Wittgenstein may have come to reject his earlier philosophy. During a heated discussion with Wittgenstein, the Italian economist Pierro Sraffa made a Neapolitan gesture of contempt, brushing his fingers outward under his chin and subsequently demanding: 'What is the logical form of *that*?' This graphic criticism may have led Wittgenstein to reject his earlier view that language served solely to picture facts. At any rate, from this point onwards, Wittgenstein's philosophy strives to show the great variety of forms of language and, indeed, the relation of language to gestures and expressive behaviour.

From 1929 Wittgenstein's re-engagement was passionate and intense. Though he published no books during this period, he wrote copiously, ensuring that there has been a steady stream of posthumously released works. In addition to writing, Wittgenstein also lectured on philosophy, and the style of these lectures has become famous. Witness Theodore Redpath's description of his first experience of these sessions:

> There must have been about two dozen people in the room, some standing, some sitting, either on deck-chairs with light-green canvas material backs, or on upright garden chairs with similar green material backs and seats. Everyone was waiting for five o'clock, when the lecture was due to start. On the mantelshelf, on which there was a small blackboard, I noticed a dark blue octavo book with the spine turned towards the audience. On the spine in gold letters were the words *Augustinus: Confessiones*. Wittgenstein himself was sitting on one of the deckchairs near the stone mantelshelf. He was bent forward, with his elbows resting on his knees and his hands pressed against each other as if he were praying. He was looking slightly downwards, and I noticed the fine form of his eyelids . . . When, on the dot of five, he sprang to his feet and, resting an arm on the mantelshelf, turned to his audience and began the lecture, one was impressed by the alertness of his face and the intense gaze of his clear blue eyes.[16]

Wittgenstein's lectures did not follow the pattern of a typical university lecture. Rather than delivering a prepared lecture, Wittgenstein would *think* out loud for a whole two hours, struggling with a philosophical problem and requesting the assistance of other people. As one can imagine, students did not always leave the room enlightened. 'Sometimes something happens, sometimes it doesn't,' I. A. Richards remarked to Redpath.[17] The tortured nature of Wittgenstein's deliberations during these lectures is apparent from his outbursts when his thoughts encountered difficulties, outbursts such as: 'You have a dreadful teacher!'; 'I'm a fool!'; 'Help me, someone!'; and 'Damn my bloody soul!' It was, however, through this strenuous mental effort that Wittgenstein arrived at a philosophical resting place entirely different from the theory of the *Tractatus*; a position which receives its most perfect expression in the pages of his late masterpiece, the *Philosophical Investigations*.

In part, this later work functions as a sustained attack on the presumptions of the *Tractatus*, and its positive views on the nature of language and meaning emerge from Wittgenstein's critique of his earlier views. The *Investigations* begins with an extended quotation from Augustine's *Confessions*, the book spied by Redpath on Wittgenstein's mantelshelf. In the quotation, Augustine documents how he came as an infant to learn language:

> When they (my elders) named some object, and accordingly moved towards something, I saw this and I grasped that the thing was called by the sound they uttered when they meant to point it out. Their intention was shewn by their bodily movements, as it were the natural language of all peoples: the expression of the face, the play of the eyes, the movement of other parts of the body, and the tone of voice which expresses our state of mind in seeking, having, rejecting, or avoiding something. Thus, as I heard words repeatedly used in their proper places in various sentences, I gradually learnt to understand what objects they signified; and after I had trained my mouth to form these signs, I used them to express my own desires. (PI §1)[18]

It is this picture which serves as the focus of Wittgenstein's attention. Augustine's words, he says,

> give us a particular picture of the essence of human language. It is this: the individual words in language name objects – sentences are combinations of such names. – In this picture of language we find the roots of the following idea: Every word has a meaning. This meaning is correlated with the word. It is the object for which the word stands. (PI §1)

What Wittgenstein finds in this Augustinian picture is a less sophisticated version of that view of language which received greater elaboration in the pages of the *Tractatus*. His main criticism of this picture is not that it is entirely wrong, but that it gives us a distorted image by ignoring the many other ways in which language functions. In order to show this, Wittgenstein imagines two primitive forms of language (which he calls 'language-games'). In §2, he describes a language for which Augustine's description is correct:

> The language is meant to serve for communication between a builder A and an assistant B. A is building with building-stones: there are blocks, pillars, slabs and beams. B has to pass the stones, and that in the order in which A needs them. For this purpose they use a language consisting of the words 'block', 'pillar', 'slab', 'beam'. A calls them out;–B brings the stone which he has learnt to bring at such-and-such a call. (PI §2)

Here words perform the task set them by Augustine and by the author of the *Tractatus*: they name objects, the object being their meaning. Contrast that language-game with the one presented by Wittgenstein in §1:

> I send someone shopping. I give him a slip marked 'five red apples'. He takes the slip to the shopkeeper, who opens the drawer marked 'apples'; then he looks up the

word 'red' in a table and finds a colour sample opposite it; then he says the series of
cardinal numbers – I assume that he knows them by heart – up to the word 'five'
and for each number he takes an apple of the same colour as the sample out of the
drawer. (PI §1)

The purpose of this language-game is to exhibit the various and multiple
ways in which words function. Although the language-game consists only
of three words, it is clear that the words 'five', 'red' and 'apples' play roles
of very different kinds. True, the word 'apple' refers to an object, but
'five'? As Wittgenstein himself asks, 'What is the meaning of the word
"five"? – No such thing was in question here, only how the word "five" is
used' (PI §1).

The lesson of the contrasting language-games is instructive. The
language-game in §1 presents a conception of words as diverse, whereas
in §2 the function of the words is uniform. The same contrast, Wittgenstein maintains, holds between Augustine's uniform conception and the
actual variety of word usage in natural language.

> Augustine, we might say, does describe a system of communication; only not
> everything that we call language is this system. And one has to say this in many
> cases where the question arises 'Is this an appropriate description or not?' The
> answer is: 'Yes, it is appropriate, but only for this narrowly circumscribed region,
> not for the whole of what you were claiming to describe.'
>
>   It is as if someone were to say: 'A game consists in moving objects about on a
> surface according to certain rules . . .' – and we replied: You seem to be thinking of
> board games, but there are others. You can make your definition correct by
> expressly restricting it to those games. (PI §3)

Here one is automatically reminded of the Tractarian claim that the
entirety of meaningful language *is* the totality of the propositions of
natural science. For the later Wittgenstein, this was purely an act of
scientific imperialism, as mistaken as the idea that cricket is not a game
because it is not played on a board.

What Wittgenstein is thus doing in the first sections of the *Investigations*
is to challenge the presuppositions of the *Tractatus* and to point the way to a
revised understanding of language. We have a tendency, he says, to think
that the meaning of a word must correspond to some thing, some object.
That intuition is challenged when we are faced with a simple language-
game such as that presented in §1. As there is no point asking to what the
word 'five' refers, our presumption about the essentially referential nature
of words will be jettisoned. Studying the application of such a word as 'five'
in a primitive language-game will 'cure you of the temptation to look about
you for some object which you might call "the meaning" ' (BB 1). And it is
not just number-words for which this is the case:

> Water!
> Away!
> Ow!
> Help!
> Fine!
> No!

Are you inclined still to call these words 'names of objects'? (PI §27)

In place of the idea that the function of words is unvaryingly to refer to objects, Wittgenstein now puts forward an alternative conception: words are analogous to *tools*:

> Think of the tools in a tool-box: there is a hammer, pliers, a saw, a screw-driver, a rule, a glue-pot, glue, nails and screws. – The functions of words are as diverse as the functions of these objects. (PI §11)

Sentences are conceived in a comparable way. If a word is a tool, then a sentence is an 'instrument' (PI §421). Likewise, 'Language is an instrument. Its concepts are instruments' (PI §569).

The tool analogy serves two crucial purposes. First, it serves to cut off the attempt to construct a 'general form' of language, the attempt to assimilate words and sentences to one another. Hence:

> Imagine someone's saying: '*All* tools serve to modify something. Thus the hammer modifies the position of the nail, the saw the shape of the board, and so on.' – And what is modified by the rule, the glue-pot, the nails? – 'Our knowledge of a thing's length, the temperature of the glue, and the solidity of the box.' – Would anything be gained by this assimilation of expressions? – (PI §14)

Time and again in the later philosophy, we encounter Wittgenstein's great emphasis on the motley character of language. He is not, *à la* the *Tractatus*, embarked on uncovering the general form of language, but is, rather, intent on surveying all the different forms that language takes. This finds explicit statement in §23:

> Review the multiplicity of language-games in the following examples, and in others:
>   Giving orders, and obeying them –
>   Describing the appearance of an object, or giving its measurements –
>   Constructing an object from a description (a drawing) –
>   Reporting an event –
>   Speculating about an event –
>   Forming and testing a hypothesis –
>   Presenting the results of an experiment in tables and diagrams –
>   Making up a story; and reading it –
>   Play-acting –
>   Singing catches –

Guessing riddles –
Making a joke; telling it –
Solving a problem in practical arithmetic –
Translating from one language into another –
Asking, thanking, cursing, greeting, praying.
– It is interesting to compare the multiplicity of the tools in language and of the
ways they are used, the multiplicity of kinds of word and sentence, with what
logicians have said about the structure of language. (Including the author of the
Tractatus Logico-Philosophicus.)

It should by now be clear how different this later view is from Wittgenstein's earlier conjectures. In the place of one monolithic thing which served solely to depict facts, the later conception of language is of something far less homogeneous. 'Language is not defined for us as an arrangement fulfilling a definite purpose. Rather 'language' is for us a name for a collection' (Z §322).

The second important aspect of the tool analogy is its relation to one of the great dictums of Wittgenstein's late work. If one is asked what the meaning of a tool is, the answer will be put in terms of the tool's specific and peculiar *use*. If we are thus to look on a sentence as an instrument, then we should look 'at its sense as its employment' (PI §421). It is reported that when asked at the Cambridge Moral Sciences Club what the meaning of a word was, Wittgenstein responded, 'Don't ask for the meaning, ask for the use.'[19] Given the later work's uncompromising stance against blanket statements, even this seems too much of a generalisation. In the *Investigations* Wittgenstein is more measured:

For a *large* class of cases – though not for all – in which we employ the word
'meaning' it can be defined thus: the meaning of a word is its use in the language.
(PI §43)

To define meaning in terms of employment is to reject the idea that words and sentences always refer to objects and facts. Rather, to discover what a person means when they utter something we need to discern what they are trying to achieve when they say it, to what use the sentence is being put. With this notion of 'meaning-as-use', Wittgenstein has moved fully away from the Tractarian model of words as labels attached to things and has instead arrived at a more dynamic model of language.

These features of Wittgenstein's later view of language are encapsulated in a prominent motif of the *Investigations*: the analogy drawn between *language* and a *game*. It is said that Wittgenstein was watching a game of football when the thought struck him that *we play games with words*. To this end he writes:

> We are talking about the spatial and temporal phenomenon of language, not about some non-spatial, non-temporal phantasm . . . But we talk about it as we do about the pieces in chess when we are stating the rules of the game, not describing their physical properties.
>
> The question 'What is a word really?' is analogous to 'What is a piece in chess?' (PI §108)

In this example, the idea of meaning-as-use is paramount. The meaning of a chess-piece is not explained by pointing to some thing which exists outside the game (as if we were to say 'The piece with the crown goes proxy for Edward II'). No, its meaning is shown by its use; by the moves it can make in accordance with the *rules* of the game. Other features of games are important here. The rules of any game are arbitrary (though binding on the players once put in place); the game should not be judged on whether it is a mirror of reality (it would make no sense to ask how successfully cricket refers to the world); nor should any game be judged according to the standards of another game (as though poker was inferior to sprinting because it was slower); hence each game has rules, standards and aims of its own. When, therefore, Wittgenstein views language as a game, he is not trying to say that language is frivolous but rather that it shares important similarities with a game. Principally, the meaning of a word (or of a sentence) is its use within a rule-governed activity, a language-game which should not be judged solely on its success in depicting the empirical world.

The game analogy serves also to highlight one great contention of Wittgenstein's later philosophy. As we have previously had cause to note, he wants to stress that language has no 'general form' and is, rather, a 'collection'. Meeting head-on the challenge that he has failed to isolate the essence of language, he contends that linguistic phenomena 'have no one thing in common . . . but that they are *related* to one another in many different ways' (PI §65).

> Consider for example the proceedings that we call 'games'. I mean board-games, card-games, ball-games, Olympic games, and so on. What is common to them all? – Don't say: 'There *must* be something common, or they would not be called "games" ' – but *look and see* whether there is anything common to all. – For if you look at them you will not see something that is common to *all*, but similarities, relationships, and a whole series of them at that. To repeat: don't think, but look! – Look for example at board-games, with their multifarious relationships. Now pass to card-games; here you find many correspondences with the first group, but many common features drop out, and others appear. When we pass next to ball-games, much that is common is retained, but much is lost. – Are they all 'amusing'? Compare chess with noughts and crosses. Or is there always winning and losing, or competition between players? Think of patience. In ball games there is winning and losing; but when a child throws his ball at the wall and catches it again, this feature

has disappeared. Look at the parts played by skill and luck; and at the difference between skill in chess and skill in tennis. Think now of games like ring-a-ring-a-roses; here is the element of amusement, but how many other characteristic features have disappeared! And we can go through the many, many other groups of games in the same way; can see how similarities crop up and disappear. (PI §66)

The result of this careful examination of games is that we detect 'a complicated network of similarities overlapping and criss-crossing' (PI §66).

I can think of no better expression to characterize these similarities than 'family resemblances'; for the various resemblances between members of a family: build, features, colour of eyes, gait, temperament, etc. etc. overlap and criss-cross in the same way. – And I shall say: 'games' form a family. (PI §67)

The family resemblance motif is an attack upon what Wittgenstein called the 'craving for generality' (BB 17). The author of the *Tractatus* had failed to recognise the immense diversity within language and had mistakenly presumed that one small segment of language – scientific language – comprised the *entirety* of language. For the later Wittgenstein this was absurd: it was like saying that all games were cricket. Just as cricket is but one example of the multifarious phenomena we call 'games', so scientific discourse is just one instance of the limitlessly extendable collection of practices gathered together under the heading 'language'.

The characterisation of language as a practice (or an activity), rather than as the 'phantasm' presented in the *Tractatus*, highlights what Wittgenstein came to see as its essentially *social* nature. As he says, 'the term "language-*game*" is meant to bring into prominence the fact that the *speaking* of language is part of an activity, or of a form of life' (PI §23). What is meant by a 'form of life' is the subject of some controversy and will be addressed in a later chapter, but Wittgenstein on one occasion equated the notion with a 'culture',[20] which suggests that language gains its significance only within something collective, like a society (or a culture). Sociological considerations were entirely lacking from the framework of the *Tractatus*. In the *Investigations* such considerations assume a position of prominence.

This collective, sociological sense arises also in Wittgenstein's late conception of the human person. Return for a moment to the Augustinian picture which begins the *Investigations*. Augustine describes not only a concept of language, but also a concept of how a child *learns* language. The child Augustine, before he can speak, peers out into the world and observes adults moving around, pointing towards things and uttering sounds, and makes the appropriate connections between what is being said and what is being pointed to. Wittgenstein comments:

> Someone coming into a strange country will sometimes learn the language of the inhabitants from ostensive definitions that they give him; and he will often have to *guess* the meaning of these definitions; and will guess sometimes right, sometimes wrong.
>
> And now, I think, we can say: Augustine describes the learning of human language as if the child came into a strange country and did not understand the language of the country; that is, as if it already had a language, only not this one. Or again: as if the child could already *think*, only not yet speak. And 'think' would here mean something like 'talk to itself'. (PI §32)

There is much that Wittgenstein objects to in Augustine's analysis,[21] but what I want principally to note here is that he reacts sternly against the *dualist* assumptions of this picture of language-learning. Dualism holds that a human person consists of both a body and a soul, and that what is essential about the person is the immaterial aspect, the body being something like a machine in which the soul is lodged. Augustine's words implicitly contain this doctrine: within the infant Augustine's little body is a soul or mind which has found itself embodied in the world. The soul can 'already think' but without the medium of language the infant Augustine's thoughts are private, screened from others.

Wittgenstein attacks Augustine's dualist assumptions on a number of fronts. First, he criticises the idea that there could be a 'private language' antecedent to the learning of one's mother tongue. Language for Wittgenstein is an essentially public thing, which gains its meaning and significance only within a shared form of life. Because language is fundamentally social, there could be no need for a single individual – someone who has never been in contact with other human beings – to have a language. Hence, before it has been taught to speak, the child will certainly not 'talk to itself'.

A second objection is to the notion that a person's thoughts and feelings – the contents of their mental life – are inaccessible to anyone but themselves. Wittgenstein wholeheartedly rejects the idea that a person's innermost thoughts are always hidden from us:

> If I see someone writhing in pain with evident cause I do not think: all the same, his feelings are hidden from me. (PI p. 223)

Of course, people do often hide their true feelings; many of us are expert liars. And people often pretend, say, to be in pain so as to gain sympathy. But Wittgenstein's point is that such dissimulation is a later, sophisticated development. Unlike the dualist, who thinks that it is in our very nature that our emotions are hidden by the body, Wittgenstein in his later work constantly stresses the natural expressiveness of the body. We *learn* how to disguise our feelings; we *learn* how to lie. Hence his illuminating question: 'Why can't a dog simulate pain? Is he too honest?' (PI §250).

Uppermost in Wittgenstein's attack upon the dualist theory is his feeling that it perverts our natural, everyday experience of other people. In the course of our lives we do not encounter immaterial minds trapped within gross bodies. No, we encounter flesh and blood creatures with whom we can immediately engage. The ethereal nature of the dualist doctrine is not just implausible and perverse, however. Wittgenstein finds it utterly dehumanising:

> The delightful way the various parts of a human body differ in temperature.

> It is humiliating to have to appear like an empty tube which is simply inflated by a mind. (CV 11)

In these remarks we encounter the marked sensuousness of Wittgenstein's philosophy, a sensuousness as striking as that of Feuerbach or of D. H. Lawrence when the latter contrasts the sterility of the mental with the vibrancy of 'blood-consciousness'.[22] Throughout his later work Wittgenstein is keen to stress the animality of the human person and the role of instinct in human life. Hence:

> I want to regard man here as an animal; as a primitive being to which one grants instinct but not ratiocination. (OC §475)

Similarly, language is not, as Augustine's conjectures imply, a mechanism designed by a rational mind in order to communicate with other beings. Rather, it has its origins in instinct:

> The origin and the primitive form of the language-game is a reaction; only from this can more complicated forms develop.
>   Language – I want to say – is a refinement, 'in the beginning was the deed'. (CV 31)

As we will subsequently discern, this vision of human beings as instinctive and passionate creatures is pivotal in Wittgenstein's account of the religious life of humanity.

One thing which is crucial to note about Wittgenstein's thoughts on the nature of the human person is the way he distances himself from traditional philosophical positions, which he sees as perverting our natural viewpoint. And it would indeed be an oversight were we not to explore in a little detail Wittgenstein's conception of the nature of philosophy itself.

The value of philosophy has been described in many ways. Plato, for example, urged that it alone could give us knowledge of ultimate reality. It was only by turning away from the illusions presented by the senses that one could arrive at an understanding of the way things really are. Other philosophers, notably John Locke, contend that the task of philosophy is to act as an 'underlabourer', clearing away some of the rubbish that stands in the way of scientific knowledge. As a third possibility, Bertrand Russell held that the value of philosophy lay not in its ability to provide firm answers to speculative questions, but rather in its ability to 'enlarge our thoughts' and keep alive our sense of wonder at the universe.[23]

Wittgenstein's conception of philosophy is as radical a departure from such views as could possibly be imagined. Rather than comprising an account of reality, rather than opening our eyes, rather, even, than clearing away misunderstandings, philosophy as traditionally practised is itself a form of misunderstanding. As he says in the preface to the *Tractatus*, philosophical problems arise when 'the logic of our language is misunderstood' (TLP p. 3). That analysis of the origins of philosophy continues into the later period. There, Wittgenstein is keen to show that language, although it works perfectly well in everyday use, is the source of our difficulties when we are doing philosophy. This robs philosophy of much of its value. Witness:

> Philosophic puzzles are irrelevant to our every-day life. They are puzzles of *language*. Instinctively we use language rightly; but to the intellect this use is a puzzle. (WLL 1)

An example of this linguistically-generated philosophical puzzlement is the desire – exemplified by the *Tractatus* itself – to link words with objects. Because we tend to think that words function as names of things, consideration of abstract nouns leads into typical philosophical questions such as 'what is time?', 'what is being?', 'what is a number?', and so on. A glance at the titles of existentialist books reveals the extent to which words like 'being' and 'nothingness' are often taken to have referents. Karl Barth's discussion of '*das Nichtige*' in his *Church Dogmatics* is likewise peppered with striking grammatical confusions:

> That which God renounces and abandons in virtue of His decision is not merely nothing. It is nothingness, and has as such its own being, albeit malignant and perverse . . . Not only what God wills, but what He does not will, is potent, *and must have a real correspondence*. What really corresponds to that which God does not will is nothingness.[24]

Here we have an entire theistic doctrine spun out of a purely linguistic misunderstanding. Barth has been bewitched by language, bewitched into thinking that the word 'nothing' *must* refer to *something*. It is as though one demanded to *see* nothing, to touch it, or feel it. Confusions such as these are the result of paying attention only to the *appearance* of words and sentences (what Wittgenstein calls 'surface grammar') rather than what is of real significance: their usage (or 'depth grammar').

In everyday discourse we never encounter such difficulties. It is only when we are outside normal linguistic activities (say, when we are in the philosophy seminar room) that we forget how language normally functions and are led into this kind of confusion. Wittgenstein's conception of language, remember, is that it performs practical, everyday tasks. Philosophy is divorced from any practical activity. Hence, 'The confusions which occupy us arise when language is like an engine idling, not when it is doing work' (PI §132). Again, 'philosophical problems arise when language *goes on holiday*' (PI §38). Here one encounters the great emphasis Wittgenstein places on the primacy of the everyday over and above the speciousness of philosophy.

This comes out most strongly in his criticism of the Tractarian method of analysis. Wittgenstein had there contended that in order perfectly to understand a proposition one had first to understand the factual situation which it represented, and then to understand how that fact was constructed (ultimately) out of simple atomic objects. Wittgenstein is here, in a sense, contrasting the understanding of ordinary people with the superior understanding of philosophers and logicians. This is not an uncommon opinion among philosophers. G. E. Moore, for example, held that there were three ways of defining any thing (a horse, say). One way would be an arbitrary verbal definition. A second would be something like a dictionary definition. A third definition would be that provided by the philosopher and would show how (and out of what) the horse was composed. Such a philosophical definition is infinitely superior to the other two. Once you have this definition, you will not only *know* more about a horse and its composition: you will understand the word better when it is spoken by someone. In the *Investigations*, Wittgenstein is dismissive of that kind of analysis and ridicules the idea that a better understanding is gained by means of it:

> When I say: 'My broom is in the corner', – is this really a statement about the broomstick and the brush? . . . Suppose that, instead of saying 'Bring me the broom', you said 'Bring me the broomstick and the brush which is fitted on to it.'! – Isn't the answer: 'Do you want the broom? Why do you put it so oddly?' (PI §60)

Here the philosopher is seen, not as the linguistic expert envisaged by Moore, but simply as an annoyance and a pedant.[25]

Philosophical problems are, then, confusions rather than genuine problems. As such they cannot be solved and should instead be *dissolved*. And this act of dissolution is achieved by *reminding* us of the everyday, practical employment (the depth grammar) of philosophically problematic language:

> When philosophers use a word – 'knowledge', 'being', 'object', 'I', 'proposition', 'name' – and try to grasp the *essence* of the thing, one must always ask oneself: is the word ever actually used in this way in the language-game which is its original home? –
> What *we* do is to bring words back from their metaphysical to their everyday use.
> (PI §116)

Wittgenstein's desire is to '*command a clear view* of the use of our words' (PI §122), to obtain what he calls a 'perspicuous representation' of language. This representation will give us an understanding of the diverse uses of words and sentences, and bring clarity to philosophical problems. 'But this simply means that the philosophical problems should *completely* disappear' (PI §133). We are then left with the striking fact that the principal philosopher of the twentieth century was intent upon the dissolution of philosophy and the destruction of its central problems, conceived as no more than 'houses of cards' (PI §118). Hence the words which could well act as an epitaph: 'I destroy, I destroy, I destroy –' (CV 21).

On his return to Cambridge, then, Wittgenstein had set about overturning the doctrines of his early philosophy and, indeed, criticising the very roots of philosophy itself. This was an eventful period of his life, in which Wittgenstein planned to settle in the Soviet Union but instead succeeded Moore to become Professor of Philosophy at Cambridge. The year was 1939 and the attainment of the professorship assisted him in his quest for British citizenship after the Anschluss had made it dangerous for a Jew to be an inhabitant of Austria. Despite the prestige of a university chair, Wittgenstein was never fully happy as a professor and continually sought work of a non-philosophical nature (and, indeed, urged his brightest students to pursue manual labour instead of academic careers). During the second world war, Wittgenstein had the opportunity to do precisely this, when he worked as a porter at Guy's Hospital in London. When the war ended he soon extricated himself from Cambridge, living for a while in Ireland until 1949, when he was diagnosed as having cancer of the prostate. He continued working on philosophy until two days before his death, on 29 April 1951. His final words are poignant: 'Tell them I've had a wonderful life!'

Though Wittgenstein's life was certainly a remarkable one, it is surprising to hear those last words. For it seems that he spent his days between torment and depression, deeply struggling both with the problems of philosophy and the problems of his own troubled soul.[26] And yet such a life was for Wittgenstein the ideal. He was impressed by a story of a friend of Beethoven who had called at the great composer's door and heard him

> 'cursing, howling and singing' over his new fugue; after a whole hour Beethoven at last came to the door, looking as if he had been fighting the devil, and having eaten nothing for 36 hours because his cook and parlour-maid had been away from his rage. That's the sort of man to be.[27]

And that was indeed 'the sort of man' Wittgenstein became: a man who *lived* his work; a man who made even his closest friends fearful of his rage; and a man who produced work of an extraordinary and lasting value, not least in the sphere of religion, to which we shall now turn.

NOTES

1. G. E. Moore, 'Wittgenstein's Lectures in 1930–33', in his *Philosophical Papers* (London: George Allen & Unwin, 1959), p. 323.
2. Hermine Wittgenstein, 'My Brother Ludwig', in R. Rhees (ed.), *Recollections of Wittgenstein* (Oxford: Oxford University Press, 1984), p. 1.
3. Wittgenstein, quoted in Brian McGuinness, *Wittgenstein: A Life* (London: Duckworth, 1988), p. 52.
4. Bertrand Russell, quoted in Ray Monk, *Ludwig Wittgenstein: The Duty of Genius* (London: Vintage, 1991), pp. 46 and 43 respectively.
5. Hermine Wittgenstein, 'My Brother Ludwig', p. 2.
6. Russell, quoted in Monk, *Ludwig Wittgenstein*, p. 91.
7. Hermine Wittgenstein, 'My Brother Ludwig', p. 3.
8. The quotations are in Rush Rhees, 'Postscript', in *Recollections of Wittgenstein*, p. 194. More material from Wittgenstein's war diaries can be found in McGuinness, *Wittgenstein: A Life*, pp. 212–66.
9. Quoted in Rhees, 'Postscript', pp. 196–97.
10. References to the *Tractatus* will be to proposition numbers. The *Tractatus* is divided into a set of numbered remarks, which function as amplifications of seven central propositions, numbered 1, 2, 3, 4, 5, 6 and 7. The greater the importance of a remark, the less decimal places it is assigned (so that, e.g., 4.1 is seen as more central than 4.1241).
11. At 4.016, Wittgenstein suggests that alphabetic script 'developed out of [hieroglyphics] without losing what was essential to depiction'.
12. The world is defined as the totality of 'facts' rather than of 'things' because the totality of things could constitute a variety of possible worlds depending upon their arrangement. It is a *specific arrangement* of things that constitutes our world.
13. C. K. Ogden's translation of these last words is more famous (and, indeed, more poetic): 'Whereof one cannot speak, thereof one must be silent.'
14. Wittgenstein, quoted in Monk, p. 228.

15. See Kimberley Cornish, *The Jew of Linz* (London: Century, 1998), pp. 40–87. On the significance of the Brouwer lecture, see P. M. S. Hacker's revised edition of *Insight and Illusion* (Oxford: Oxford University Press, 1986), pp. 120–8.

16. Theodore Redpath, *Ludwig Wittgenstein: A Student's Memoir* (London: Duckworth, 1990), pp. 17–18.

17. Ibid., p. 19.

18. References to passages from the *Philosophical Investigations* are in the form of paragraph – rather than page – numbers. This applies to other of the later works also, and is signified by §. Here the numbering system is less complex than that of the *Tractatus*, paragraphs flowing in one whole-number sequence.

19. John Wisdom, 'Ludwig Wittgenstein, 1934–1937', in *Paradox and Discovery* (Oxford: Basil Blackwell, 1965), p. 87.

20. This connection between a form of life and a culture can be discerned by attention to an early draft of the remark in the *Investigations* that 'to imagine a language means to imagine a form of life' (PI §19). In the *Brown Book* the thought was formulated thus: 'We could also easily imagine a language (and that means again a culture) . . .' (BB 134).

21. Of particular significance might be Wittgenstein's objection to the idea of *ostensive definition* (that is, to the notion that the meanings of words are learned via a gesture of pointing combined with the use of such words as 'This is called *x*'). Wittgenstein wants to challenge the implication of Augustine's picture that ostensive definition constitutes the very foundation of language-learning. For how could someone unacquainted with the process of ostensive definition know that what was being pointed to was the object itself? Why not the colour of the object, the function of the object, a command to do something with the object? In other words, in order to understand the dynamics of ostensive definition one must already understand the language-game it constitutes; one must already therefore be a language-user. On these points see *Philosophical Investigations*, §§27–38.

22. J. T. Boulton, *The Letters of D. H. Lawrence* (Cambridge: Cambridge University Press, 1979), vol. I, p. 503.

23. For each of these approaches to the nature of philosophy, see: Plato's *Republic* (Harmondsworth: Penguin, 1955) ('The Simile of the Cave'); John Locke, *An Essay Concerning Human Understanding* (Oxford: Oxford University Press, 1979) ('The Epistle to the Reader'); and Bertrand Russell, *The Problems of Philosophy* (Oxford: Oxford University Press, 1912) (ch. 15, 'The Value of Philosophy').

24. Karl Barth, *Church Dogmatics* (Edinburgh: T. & T. Clark, 1960), vol. III, pt 3, p. 352 (emphasis added).

25. The atomistic desire to resolve propositions and facts into their simple constituents comes under sustained attack in the *Investigations*. Wittgenstein's principal objection is that there is no single, context-independent distinction between what is complex and what is simple. At §47, therefore, he asks, 'What are the simple constituent parts of a chair?' Is it all the separate pieces of wood which are fitted together? Or is it the atoms which compose the wood? Or is it the chair itself? Our answer will depend on the circumstances we are in and what we want to know. 'Simple objects' will mean one thing to the carpenter building a chair, another thing to the molecular scientist, and yet another thing altogether to the interior designer imposing minimalism on a room. Such reflections lead Wittgenstein to say: 'We use the word "composite" (and therefore the word "simple") in an enormous number of different and differently related ways', and that therefore it 'makes no sense at all to speak absolutely of the "simple parts of a chair" ' (PI §47).

26. Witness Russell's memorable account of the young Wittgenstein: 'He used to come to my rooms at midnight and, for hours, he would walk backwards and forwards like a caged

tiger. On arrival, he would announce that when he left my rooms he would commit suicide. So in spite of getting sleepy, I did not like to turn him out. On one such evening, after an hour or two of dead silence, I said to him, "Wittgenstein, are you thinking about logic or about your sins?" "Both," he said, and then reverted to silence' ('Philosophers and Idiots', *The Listener*, 55, February 1955, p. 247).
27. Quoted in Monk, *Ludwig Wittgenstein*, p. 45.

2

THE MYSTICAL

In the *Tractatus*, Wittgenstein had offered an account of language which stressed its essentially *pictorial* character. The task of language is, purely and simply, to describe the facts we encounter in the world in which we find ourselves. A proposition gains its sense from being a linguistic representation of a possible or an actual factual state of affairs. If an utterance does not fulfil this pictorial requirement, if it does not possess this relation to the world, then that utterance can be neither true nor false, but is, rather, devoid of any meaning whatsoever. This, as we saw, enables Wittgenstein to dispense with metaphysics. A form of discourse which does not function as a straightforward description of the world as we find it, but which attempts in some fashion to extend beyond the world of experience, has 'failed to give a meaning to certain signs in its propositions'; it has failed, that is, adequately to connect language to reality.

In the previous chapter we saw how the framework of the *Tractatus* dispensed not just with metaphysics but also with the language of aesthetics and of ethics. Religion, too, is not immune from this attack. Like metaphysics, the language of theology is not possessed of the logic which permits sense. To take but one example, a Christian theologian may on occasion put forward and defend the trinitarian formula that 'God is three persons in one being'. And indeed many Christians may firmly hold this belief. But when exposed to the exacting criteria of meaning elaborated in the *Tractatus*, the trinitarian formula can be seen to lack sense. Language only has sense if its component parts (words) can be connected with reality, but in the case of such theological language we cannot even begin to connect those words with the objects found in the world, and thus cannot hope to compare theological propositions with reality in order to ascertain their truth-value (TLP 4.05). So it is not that the formula of the Trinity is false. No, it is entirely meaningless.

What could be found, then, in the *Tractatus* was a new weapon in the criticism of religion. When previous philosophers had wanted to cast doubt on religion, the task was generally that of demonstrating that it was false, that there were no realities corresponding to the objects of worship as traditionally conceived. This kind of project can most explicitly be seen in the writings of David Hume. Hume picks apart the arguments intended by theologians to prove the existence of God, condemning, for example, the theistic contention that, just as the existence of a watch with its orderly and purposive nature entails the postulation of a watchmaker, so the orderly and purposive character of the world entails a divine designer. Hume shows how such an argument rests on grave errors: the world is nothing like a watch, so need not have been designed; the world is equally probably the product of chance rather than design; a belief in the Christian God would not flow from an acceptance of the designedness of the world; and so on. And as well as resting on only the shakiest of rational foundations, there is much evidence to be garnered indicating the downright *falsity* of religious belief. Here Hume appeals both to the problem of evil, contending that the existence of a loving, all-powerful god is incompatible with the undeniable reality of suffering, and to the history of religion, showing how it is rooted, not in a rational contemplation of the world, but in fear, ignorance and superstition. Having, then, engaged in an assessment of the evidence for and against the truth of religion, Hume's (implied) conclusion is that religion is almost certainly false.[1]

The critique of religion found in the *Tractatus* is not of this kind. Wittgenstein does not waste time garnering evidence for the falsity of religion. Rather, he focuses upon the *discourse* of religion and shows how it lacks the pictorial relation to the world essential for the possession of meaning. Religious language does not even get so far as to be false: because of our inability to show how (e.g.) the word 'God' goes proxy for an object in the world, all sentences containing that word are devoid of sense. The debate about religion ceases, then, to be about whether religion is true or false. It is neither: it is senseless.

Though Wittgenstein's challenge to the meaningfulness of religion was radical and original, it was not entirely without precedents in the history of the criticism of religion. Ludwig Feuerbach, for example, who famously contended that God is nothing other than human nature magnified and projected outwards, based his atheism partly upon the yawning chasm existing between those statements ceaselessly made about God – that he is omnipotent, omniscient, creator of the universe, loving, and so on – and the complete lack of *evidence* in favour of those claims.[2] This appeal to the necessity of evidence not just in order to establish truth but to establish *meaning* is found in embryonic form in Hume's *Enquiry Concerning Human Understanding*, where Hume famously writes:

If we take in our hand any volume; of divinity or school metaphysics, for instance; let us ask, *Does it contain any abstract reasoning concerning quantity or number?* No. *Does it contain any experimental reasoning concerning matter of fact and existence?* No. Commit it then to the flames: for it can contain nothing but sophistry and illusion.[3]

Here the attack on the status of religious language adopts the characteristically empiricist claim that for any assertion to have meaning it must be rooted in the experience of the senses.

Though that kind of contention did not receive explicit formulation in the *Tractatus*, the picture theory of meaning was given just such an empiricist twist in the 1920s when, in collaboration with Wittgenstein, a group of philosophers dubbed the 'Vienna Circle' devised a philosophical programme which became known as Logical Positivism. According to Positivism, if a sentence was to be meaningful it had to satisfy the demands of the verification principle, which baldly states that 'the meaning of a sentence is its method of verification'. In other words, if a sentence is to be meaningful it must be capable of proof. If I say – to take a banal example – 'I am six feet tall', then this assertion is clearly verifiable (you can take a tape-measure to me) and therefore possesses meaning. And this criterion is given perfect generality by the positivists. It applies to each and every assertion. Witness Wittgenstein's own words on the matter:

If I can never verify the sense of a proposition completely, then I cannot have meant anything by the proposition either. Then the proposition signifies nothing whatsoever. (VC 47)

These rather extreme words certainly constitute what A. J. Ayer called the 'strong sense' of verifiability. According to this sense, a statement is meaningful only if it can *conclusively* be proven. Such a formulation was unworkable in practice, for it rendered meaningless many obviously significant statements. The statement 'All mice like cheese', for instance, cannot be conclusively verified, but to claim that it was a meaningless utterance would be undeniably perverse. To avoid such counter-intuitive results of verificationism, Ayer advocated instead verification in the 'weak sense': a statement 'is verifiable, in the weak sense, if it is possible for experience to render it probable'.[4] Our statement about mice will survive weak verifiability: if we were to take a random sample of mice and found that 100 per cent of that sample liked cheese, we would then be justified in saying 'All mice like cheese.' More to the point, these verification conditions guarantee the sense of the proposition, safeguarding it against any claim that it is meaningless.

The same cannot, unfortunately, be said for the characteristic utterance of religion. For Ayer, typical religious assertions are not even in principle verifiable and no sense experience can contribute anything to an enquiry into their truth or falsity. Consider again in this context the language of the Trinity: how might sense experience verify or even make probable the belief that God is three persons in one being? 'Would any observations be relevant to the determination of its truth or falsehood?'[5] Here we are entirely at a loss, and as a result are led to conclude that the language of theology is hopelessly non-informative. This stark conclusion is further compounded by the metaphysical nature of religious beliefs, for

> The term 'god' is a metaphysical term. And if 'god' is a metaphysical term, then it cannot even be probable that a god exists. For to say that 'God exists' is to make a metaphysical utterance which cannot be either true or false.[6]

Ayer is, of course, not entirely dogmatic in his consignment of religion to the realm of the nonsensical. Other common forms of discourse – such as the language of morals – are not capable of verification (for how could one *prove* that, say, stealing was wrong?) and yet Ayer is quite happy to permit the continuation of ethical discourse. This does, none the less, require a certain redefinition of what is going on when moral judgements are made. Such judgements are no longer seen as informative, so that to declare that murder is immoral is not to say anything about murder. If I state that murder is wrong, I am, according to Ayer, engaged in an *emotive* and an *autobiographical* exercise. I am telling you something about myself – that I disapprove of murder – but I am telling you nothing about the character of murder itself (in the same way that 'I don't like broccoli' tells you something about me and nothing about broccoli).

Ayer suggests that something similar might be true of religion. If, for example, someone declares of a sunset that it manifests the glory of God, that utterance need not be nonsensical. It may legitimately be regarded as a poetic statement, the 'cash-value' of which might be 'Isn't that sunset beautiful?' Here religious discourse is permitted, but only in the sense of having an emotive or poetic character. Religion is allowed back in, but at the enormous cost that it does not say anything about the world. If the religious believer goes on to say 'No, the sunset *really* is a sign of God's love for the world,' he is then talking nonsense. It is in such a fashion that Logical Positivism constituted a supremely important weapon in the arsenal of the critics of religion.

One might presume, then, given both the *Tractatus*' suppression of religious utterance and his formative influence on verificationism, that Wittgenstein shared the positivists' aggressively anti-religious attitude. A couple of factors might seem to favour this presumption. We have, to begin with, Wittgenstein's stated desire to 'cut out the transcendental twaddle'.[7] Moreover, one of Russell's first impressions of Wittgenstein was that he was militantly atheistic, being 'far more terrible with Christians than I am'.[8] The *Tractatus* might, then, be seen as an all-out attack upon religion, a piece of ferocious criticism, which, in divesting religious discourse of its significance and therefore of its claim to truthfulness, completes the sceptical work initiated by such men as Hume and Voltaire.

And yet there is much that militates against that interpretation of the *Tractatus*. One such thing is Wittgenstein's view of the limitations of verification. Witness:

> I used at one time to say that, in order to get clear how a sentence is used, it was a good idea to ask oneself the question: 'How would one try to verify such an assertion?' But that's just one way among others of getting clear about the use of a word or sentence. For example, another question which it is often very useful to ask oneself is: 'How is this word learned?' 'How would one set about teaching a child to use this word?' But some people have turned this suggestion about asking for the verification into a dogma – as if I'd been advancing a theory about meaning.[9]

So even Wittgenstein's advocacy of verification extended only so far as the advocacy of *one way* of establishing the meaning of a statement. This entails, of course, that the inability of religion to satisfy the demands of the verification principle should not automatically entail its dismissal.

More strikingly perhaps, and certainly more suggestive of religious sensibility, we have the evidence of Wittgenstein's character and pre-occupations during the first world war. A famous story tells how Wittgenstein chanced upon a bookshop in Tarnow and found that it contained only one book: Tolstoy's *The Gospel in Brief*. Buying it simply because it was the only title there, Wittgenstein became entranced by the book, reading it over and over again, and carrying it with him at all times, so markedly that other soldiers dubbed him 'the man with the gospels'. And just as Wittgenstein read avidly on religious matters so too do his written thoughts from this period manifest such concerns. Not only do phrases such as 'God give me strength', 'God is with me', and 'Amen', appear time and again in his diaries, but, more significantly, religious themes pervade his philosophical notebooks. On 11 June 1916, for example, he writes:

> What do I know about God and the purpose of life?
> I know that this world exists.
> That I am placed in it like my eye in its visual field.
> That something about it is problematic, which we call its meaning.

That this meaning does not lie in it but outside it . . .
The meaning of life, i.e. the meaning of the world, we can call God.
And connect with this the comparison of God to a father.
To pray is to think about the meaning of life. (NB 72–3)

Of course, one could easily dismiss the importance of such remarks by saying that these are the emotional blatherings of a man in a crisis. It is, after all, notoriously the case that even the most irreligious of people will often resort to prayer when faced with death.

But that kind of scepticism is only superficially plausible here. When we turn to the *Tractatus* itself, we find ample evidence that this work is not intended as a contribution to the criticism of religion. Consider, first of all, Wittgenstein's attempts after the end of the war to find a publisher for his book. Writing to one prospective publisher, Ludwig von Ficker, who specialised in works on literature and cultural criticism, Wittgenstein advertised the *Tractatus* by stating that the most important aspect of the book was not its treatment of logic and meaning. Rather, 'the point of the book is ethical' (LF 94). And indeed, even the most cursory of glances at (in particular the final pages of) the *Tractatus* reveals its author's obsession with ethical and religious questions, and illustrates that if the *Tractatus* is a work of irreligious criticism it goes about its criticism in the most bizarre of ways. Consider just this one remark:

6.432   *How* things are in the world is a matter of complete indifference for what
          is higher. God does not reveal himself *in* the world.

These words are a statement, not of radical atheism, but of radical transcendence, and are akin to the spirit, not of positivism, but of Karl Barth's emphasis on the dialectic between time and eternity, or of Kierkegaard's stress on 'the infinite qualitative distinction between God and humanity'.[10] The hiatus between such an idea and the positivist programme calls for a radically different interpretation of Wittgenstein's project than had been provided by the philosophers of the Vienna Circle, who saw the *Tractatus* as very much in tune with their own atheistic work. One might, of course, find it hard to isolate the differences between Wittgenstein and positivist philosophers. After all, their results are much the same: the factual language of the natural sciences is the sole legitimate subject of discourse, and anyone who desires to speak informatively about God (or about what is timelessly good, or beautiful) is to be chastised for talking nonsense or for failing 'to give a meaning to certain signs in his propositions'. Despite these similar results, there is, as we have already noted, a crucial difference in the tone and spirit of Wittgenstein's work, and a corresponding difference in the reasons he gives for confining religion to the category of the unsayable.

Consider first of all some words from the preface to the *Tractatus*. Having written that 'the *truth* of the thoughts that are here communicated seems to me unassailable and definitive', and that therefore he has effectively solved all the problems of philosophy, Wittgenstein then remarks:

> If I am not mistaken in this belief, then the second thing in which the value of this work consists is that it shows how little is achieved when these problems are solved. (TLP p. 4)

When one thinks of the achievements of the *Tractatus*, and the plaudits it received on its publication (and continues to receive), it is quite staggering that Wittgenstein himself should regard his book's conclusions to be of merely trivial significance. This is very much connected, once again, with themes in his correspondence with Ficker. To recall, Wittgenstein had stressed to Ficker that the *Tractatus* was a book with an 'ethical' point. In the same letter, he says this:

> I once wanted to give a few words in the foreword which now actually are not in it, which, however, I'll write to you now because they might be a key for you: I wanted to write that my work consists of two parts: of the one which is here, and of everything which I have *not* written. And precisely this second part is the important one. For the Ethical is delimited from within, as it were, by my book; and I'm convinced that, *strictly* speaking, it can ONLY be delimited in this way. In brief, I think: All of that which *many* are *babbling* today, I have defined in my book by remaining silent about it. (LF 94–5)

The idea here, then, is expressly *not* the positivist contention that non-factual discourse is worthy of ridicule. On the contrary, Wittgenstein is suggesting that those things which he has banished from the realm of meaningful language are infinitely *more important* than that which can legitimately be articulated. And he is certainly not intent upon throwing doubt on the reality of the unsayable. Hence, from the pages of the *Tractatus* itself:

> 6.522 There are, indeed, things that cannot be put into words. They *make themselves manifest*. They are what is mystical.

Here, Wittgenstein is identifying a whole realm of things and concerns – dubbed 'the mystical', and inclusive of ethical, aesthetic, and religious matters – which cannot be expressed, cannot be verbalised, and which are worthy, not of ridicule, but of the deepest respect.

All these points are memorably expressed by Paul Engelmann in his description of the discontinuity between the project of the *Tractatus* and the positivist programme:

> A whole generation of disciples was able to take Wittgenstein for a positivist because he has something of enormous importance in common with the positivists: he draws the line between what we can speak about and what we must be silent about just as they do. The difference is only that they have nothing to be silent about. Positivism holds – and this is its essence – that what we can speak about is all that matters in life. *Whereas Wittgenstein passionately believes that all that really matters in human life is precisely what, in his view, we must be silent about.* When he nevertheless takes immense pains to delimit the unimportant, it is not the coastline of that island which he is bent on surveying with such meticulous accuracy, but the boundary of the ocean.[11]

The *Tractatus*, then, was the attempt to demarcate what can be said from what cannot be said, whilst (here's the twist) contending – *contra* positivism – that the unsayable alone is important, hence consigning discursive thought and scientific language to the realm of the merely trivial.

At first sight, perhaps, Wittgenstein's injunction to silence is bizarre, in a way that the positivists' is not. Otto Neurath's verdict that 'one must indeed be silent, but not *about* anything' makes perfect sense: religious talk was for him nonsensical chatter about non-existent entities.[12] But Wittgenstein, on the other hand, has adopted no atheistic mantle, so why be silent? Indeed, if the mystical is of the utmost importance, surely we *should* talk about it. And, of course, many people *do* talk about the nature of God, or about what is good or beautiful. To say 'You cannot talk about God,' then, is not akin to saying 'You cannot make two and two equal five.' Wittgenstein is pointing, rather, to a number of factors which make the attempt to talk about such matters a hopeless and an undesirable task.

This diagnosis is informed by an amalgam of traditional and modern concerns. The *Tractatus* can be seen as the attempt to put on a sure philosophical footing ideas about humanity's relation to the godhead evident within the great religious traditions and indeed within the Bible itself. Wittgenstein's remarks on the unknowability of God (that 'God does not reveal himself in the world') are reminiscent of what we find, for example, in the book of Ecclesiastes, where it is written:

> Be not rash with your mouth, nor let your heart be hasty to utter a word before God, for God is in heaven, and you upon earth; therefore let your words be few.[13]

A comparable recognition of the infinite gulf between human language and the divine can be found in the *Tractatus*: 'Propositions can express nothing that is higher' (TLP 6.42). Just as the Jewish tradition condemns any hubristic attempt to understand or to know God ('man shall not see me and live'[14]), so Wittgenstein is cutting off any human attempt to become familiar with holy things.[15] See how this concern emerges in a remark of Wittgenstein's, related by Drury:

> I have been reading in a German author, a contemporary of Kant's, Hamann, where he says, commenting on the story of the Fall in Genesis: 'How like God to wait until the cool of the evening before confronting Adam with his transgression.' Now I wouldn't for the life of me dare to say, 'how like God'. I wouldn't claim to know how God should act.[16]

What Wittgenstein objects to, then, is a certain human tendency to extend beyond our limits, and to talk of things about which we should rightfully be silent and respectful. The *Tractatus* can thus be read as a modern *via negativa*. The picture theory of meaning, with its resultant banishment of theology to silence, is designed to protect 'what is higher' from the perverting, all-too-human encroaches of language. It is not philistinism, then, that informs Wittgenstein's silence. No, just as Kant famously 'found it necessary to deny *knowledge*, in order to make room for *faith*,'[17] so the *Tractatus* sets a limit to what can be spoken (and therefore thought) in order to respect the awesome power of the mystical.

The mechanism of this procedure emerges clearly in Wittgenstein's 'Lecture on Ethics', delivered in 1929 to a Cambridge society known as 'The Heretics'. It should be remembered here that the ethical constitutes for Wittgenstein part of the mystical, and that he describes ethics as 'the enquiry into the meaning of life' (LE 5) (just as, indeed, he had associated God with the meaning of life (cf. NB 73, 74)). Echoing the Tractarian view that 'all propositions are of equal value' (TLP 6.4), Wittgenstein continues to claim: 'There are no propositions which, in any absolute sense, are sublime, important, or trivial' (LE 6). Even the most dreadful of murders constitutes just another fact, having in itself no more significance than the falling of a stone.[18] A full description of the world would, thus, contain 'facts, facts, and facts but no Ethics' (LE 7). This entails that ethics could not be the subject of a scientific enquiry, that science cannot deal with something 'intrinsically sublime and above all other subject matters':

> I can only describe my feeling by the metaphor, that, if a man could write a book on Ethics which really was a book on Ethics, this book would, with an explosion, destroy all the other books in the world. Our words used as we use them in science, are vessels capable only of containing and conveying meaning and sense, *natural* meaning and sense. Ethics, if it is anything, is supernatural and our words will only express facts; as a teacup will only hold a teacup full of water and if I were to pour out a gallon over it. (LE 7)

This wonderful image illustrates perfectly the radical discrepancy perceived by Wittgenstein between natural language and supernatural realities. Our language is sufficient only for picturing the mundane world of facts; it is woefully inadequate to handle the glorious ineffability of the mystical, which is beyond the world, and therefore beyond words, beyond the humdrum realm of states of affairs. Wittgenstein's *via negativa* is based therefore on an acute awareness of the unknowability of 'what is higher', coupled with a compelling portrait of the nature and limits of language.

This brings us to another central and striking image. At the end of his ethics lecture, Wittgenstein considers what has caused him to spend so much time thinking about something 'beyond significant language' and hence nonsensical:

> My whole tendency and I believe the tendency of all men who ever tried to write or talk Ethics or Religion was to run against the boundaries of language. This running against the walls of our cage is perfectly, absolutely hopeless. (LE 11–12)

The notion of the thrust against the limits of language is a frequent theme in the early philosophy, and an idea which Wittgenstein links with Kierkegaard.[19] It is, he says, a perennial human urge, which he would never ridicule. Of course, given the exacting demands of the *Tractatus*, one should not speak for fear of talking nonsense, but Wittgenstein seems to think that there is a definite worth in the occasional breaking of the Tractarian silence. For although the results of the thrust against language's limits are cognitively hopeless,

> the inclination, the running up against something, *indicates something*. St. Augustine knew that already when he said: What, you swine, you want not to talk nonsense! Go ahead and talk nonsense, it does not matter! (VC 69)

As Augustine's words are more generally rendered, the great saint says, 'Yet woe to him that speaketh not, since mute are even the most eloquent.'[20] These words bear witness to the tension in mystical theology between on the one hand a recognition of the unknowability of the divine and yet on the other the compelling desire to speak about that which lies beyond human knowledge. On Wittgenstein's interpretation, this desire results in the production of speech which, though nonsensical, is somehow *important*. Our question must now be: how can that which is nonsensical also be important? And to this question, we can isolate two possible answers, which can for shorthand be called the 'anthropological' and the 'transcendental' interpretations of the category of important nonsense.

If we interpret Wittgenstein's thought on the mystical in the anthropological way, then the emphasis is placed, not on what is beyond the world, but rather on human beings themselves, on their desires and religious impulses. After all, in the 'Lecture on Ethics' Wittgenstein speaks only of 'a tendency *in the human mind*' (LE 12, emphasis added), which suggests that what he calls 'the mystical' is a creation of the human mind, rather than a genuinely transcendent reality. The question about the important nonsense generated about the mystical will now retreat to the human causes of those expressions. The emphasis might fall on how our existence here seems so futile and empty, how the world of facts fails to satisfy our deepest desires. Even the greatest accumulation of factual evidence will fall far short of answering the perennial troubled questions of human life: why are we here? what is the meaning of it all? For wherever we look, however persistently we research, whatever we read, nothing seems to quell our anxiety. Hence:

> The urge towards the mystical comes of the non-satisfaction of our wishes by science. We *feel* that even if all *possible* scientific questions are answered *our problem is still not touched at all.* (NB 51; cf. TLP 6.52)

Refuge in the mystical provides for us a way to reflect upon our lives, to come to terms with the problematic elements of our existence. But how is this achieved?

In the *Tractatus*, Wittgenstein is suggesting that 'the mystical' constitutes a particular way of looking at the world, a particular way of responding to the facts encountered there. This would appear to be the thrust of the following comments:

> 6.4321 The facts all contribute only to setting the problem, not to its solution.
> 6.44 It is not *how* things are in the world that is mystical, but *that* it exists.
> 6.45 To view the world sub specie aeterni is to view it as a whole – a limited whole.
> Feeling the world as a limited whole – it is this that is mystical.

Wittgenstein's contention that what is mystical is a view of the world *sub specie aeternitatis* requires further clarification. Literally meaning 'under the aspect of eternity', to see the world in this manner would be to turn from too narrow a focus (say, a purely self-centred one) and to widen one's view so that the entirety of the world is perceived. Once one's own petty concerns have been set aside and the world is seen in its totality, an air of significance may begin to be detected in life. It is in these terms that Wittgenstein's account of mystical experience coincides with *aesthetic* experience: just as the mystical viewpoint captures the world holistically, so a work of art is 'the object seen *sub specie aeternitatis*'; seen, that is, not from in the midst of things but 'from outside' (NB 83). The connection between the aesthetic and the mystical is crucial. In the same way that two people may have strikingly different responses to a work of art (one finds it moving and powerful, the other worthless and a disgrace), so two people may react in varying ways to the world. While one person may achieve the mystical consciousness of the world, another person may sense around them nothing of significance. Here we find the germ of a view of the contrast between the religious believer and the atheist which will survive on into Wittgenstein's later thought; and it is a contrast centred upon different ways of viewing the same reality. The clash between belief and unbelief is not a disagreement over the *facts* of the world: it is more akin to a disagreement over *aesthetic taste*.

Consider now the character of this mystical–cum–aesthetic experience. It is the existence of the world *as such*, rather than the arrangement of things within it, that is mystical. 'Aesthetically, the miracle is that the world exists. That what exists does exist' (NB 86). This idea of the world's 'miraculous' existence is central to Wittgenstein's characterisation of the mystical. It appears in his discussion of ethical experience in the 'Lecture on Ethics' and there effectively encapsulates the meaning of 'important nonsense'. Trying to express what he means by the idea of 'absolute value', Wittgenstein appeals to an experience for which this expression is suitable:

> I believe the best way of describing [this experience] is to say that when I have it *I wonder at the existence of the world*. And I am then inclined to use such phrases as 'how extraordinary that anything should exist' or 'how extraordinary that the world should exist.' I will mention another experience straight away which I also know and which others of you might be acquainted with: it is, what one might call, the experience of feeling *absolutely* safe. I mean the state of mind in which one is inclined to say 'I am safe, nothing can injure me whatever happens.' Now let me consider these experiences, for, I believe, they exhibit the very characteristics we try to get clear about. And there the first thing I have to say is, that the verbal expression which we give to these experiences is nonsense! If I say 'I wonder at the existence of the world' I am misusing language. (LE 8)

So here we have two arch-expressions of value – of the mystical – which can be shown to be nonsensical. Take first of all the idea of absolute safety. We might feel safe in our own homes, or those of us happily ensconced in the British Isles might feel safe from earthquakes, tornadoes and poisonous spiders. But this only means that it is hugely improbable that *certain things* should endanger me. What would it mean to be safe *whatever* happens? Similarly, marvelling at the existence of the world is nonsensical. I may wonder at the existence of a great number of things: a thunderstorm, perhaps, or the aurora borealis. And if I see the northern lights, I might indeed be sufficiently moved to say something like, 'Isn't it remarkable that there should be such a thing?' But then, says Wittgenstein, 'it is nonsense to say that I wonder at the existence of the world, because I cannot imagine it not existing' (LE 9). One may not be entirely convinced by this reasoning. After all, one of the great historical questions of philosophy has been 'Why is there something rather than nothing?', and it may be felt that the desire to uncover the reason for the existence of the universe is legitimate and not nonsensical. Nevertheless, the lesson Wittgenstein is trying to drive home with these examples is 'that a certain characteristic misuse of our language runs through *all* ethical and religious expressions' (LE 9).

Just four years after he wrote those words, Wittgenstein supplied a dramatic example of how religious concepts misuse language, an example which focuses on the character of the scapegoat ritual, described in the sixteenth chapter of the book of Leviticus. In this practice, a consecrated goat has the sins of the community transfered on to it and is then sent out into the wilderness, taking with it the burden of guilt. Wittgenstein comments:

> The scapegoat, on which one lays one's sins, and who runs away into the desert with them − a false picture, similar to those that cause errors in philosophy. (BT 197).[21]

The 'misuse of our language' inherent in this practice is the representation of 'sin' as though it were some kind of object that could be placed on to something (in this instance, the goat), just as one might place a basket on its back. The confusion exhibited here is thus comparable to the linguistic misunderstanding which led Karl Barth to think that 'nothingness' was *something*. Both arise from a reification of abstract nouns. Nevertheless, the scapegoat ritual reveals something rather deep and important, namely the acutely-felt sense of guilt of a community and the desire to be free from that burden. This desperate longing results in a thrust against the limits of sense, but it is nothing to be ridiculed, for it reveals in the starkest of fashions the pains and the anxiety of a human existence.

The anthropological interpretation of the thrust against the limits of language highlights, then, the deep human desires and frailties that inform religion, yet it does not necessarily posit the presence of anything *beyond* the world. The thrust is a purely human tendency. What I have called the 'transcendental' interpretation, on the other hand, senses that Wittgenstein *is* aware of a higher order of realities, and is stressing the human desire to gain communion with these realities, or at least to grasp them by means of the intellect. On this interpretation, the image of language as 'a cage' is to be taken very seriously.[22] Our predicament is akin to that of people who have never left a prison in which they were born. Denied any experience of the outside world, the only hint that there is something beyond the walls of their cage is a few cracks in the wall through which light occasionally glimmers. A longing to know that hidden world results in the elaboration of fanciful dreams with no foundation. Silence would be no less informative. The cage analogy is somewhat similar to Plato's simile of the cave, but Wittgenstein's picture is less hopeful: while one could educate oneself out of Plato's cave, there is for Wittgenstein no escape from the restrictions of language and the world. It is not just accidental, then, that we end up talking nonsense: we could do no other. But note: there is no denial (not even implicit) of the extra-human reality of the mystical. On Engelmann's analogy, we are marooned on an island, and spend our days obsessively babbling about what is beyond the horizon, something we have never known, nor can ever know – but *is there* none the less.

The mystical elements of the early philosophy may then be regarded as Wittgenstein's 'hopeless' attempts to articulate what lies beyond the world. And there are, indeed, a number of significant remarks in which Wittgenstein expresses his thoughts about the nature of God, to which we shall now turn. At the outset, however, it must be stressed that we should not expect to find a coherent and consistent philosophy of religion in these remarks. For what we here encounter are the results of Wittgenstein's personal thrust against the limits of language, and they are, to say the least, somewhat cryptic. Nevertheless, the ideas we find in both the *Tractatus* and the *Notebooks* provide a crucial insight into Wittgenstein's early thinking on God and the religious life.

We have previously seen that Wittgenstein attempted to link God with the question of life's meaning, and this connection is again pursued when he writes:

> To believe in a God means to understand the question about the meaning of life.
> To believe in a God means to see that the facts of the world are not the end of the matter.
> To believe in God means to see that life has a meaning. (NB 74)

This passage reinforces much that we earlier noted. Religious belief is intimately connected with the feeling that the facts are not enough; that there is something beyond the factual which is of the greatest significance. Like the mystical consciousness, it comes of a profound dissatisfaction with the answers provided by science. 'Understanding the question' about the meaning of life means recognising that life's meaning cannot be found *in* the world; that like God, meaning is located outside the humdrum order of facts. This connection drawn by Wittgenstein between God and the meaning of life is in some ways comparable to John Macquarrie's paraphrase of the prologue to John's Gospel, in which he substitutes 'Meaning' for 'Word' or 'Logos'. Witness:

(1) Fundamental to everything is Meaning. It is closely connected with what we call 'God', and indeed Meaning and God are virtually identical. (2) To say that God was in the beginning is to say that Meaning was in the beginning. (3) All things were made meaningful, and there was nothing made that was meaningless. (4) Life is the drive toward Meaning, and life has emerged into self-conscious humanity, as the (finite) bearer and recipient of Meaning. (5) And meaning shines out through the threat of absurdity, for absurdity has not overwhelmed it.[23]

If Wittgenstein *is* saying something like this, then his view of God may not be wildly divergent from an orthodox Christian position.

On the other hand, other of his remarks in the *Notebooks* seem far more idiosyncratic, and entail a radical departure from the Christian concept of God. In these remarks, Wittgenstein goes much further than to claim that God provides the answer to the meaning of life and the world: he now contends that God *is* the world. Such a claim suggests that Wittgenstein's early thought on religion is a form of *pantheism*, and his conception of God has close affinities with Spinoza's famous declaration that 'the Universe is God'.[24] Denying the commonly-held distinction between God and world, the pantheist holds that the world itself is divine, and Wittgenstein appears to do likewise when in the *Notebooks* he writes:

How things stand, is God.
God is, how things stand. (NB 79)

Here God is described in much the same way as the *Tractatus* defines a fact ('how things stand') or the world ('all that is the case'). It then strongly suggests that Wittgenstein is pantheistically identifying God with the world. And this identification is found elsewhere in the *Notebooks*, and principally after he has first made an observation (to be considered shortly) about our being dependent on an 'alien will'.

However this may be, at any rate we *are* in a certain sense dependent, and what we are dependent on we can call God.
    In this sense God would simply be fate, or, what is the same thing: The world – which is independent of our will. (NB 74)

These entries from the *Notebooks* show, then, in the starkest of terms, that Wittgenstein's earliest philosophy of religion was pantheistic. He is, like Spinoza, keen to make the correlation: *Deus sive Natura*.

If, however, this is the case, then Wittgenstein's pantheism seems to run counter to the only truly theological statement of the *Tractatus*, in which, as we saw, it is stressed that 'God does not reveal himself *in* the world' (TLP 6.432). Yet this can be reconciled with the doctrines of the *Notebooks*, for the God of pantheism *is* the world, so he is not *in* the world (just as the world is not in the world). Notwithstanding this particular escape route, there are certainly tensions here. Perhaps the most interesting of these tensions lies in Wittgenstein's attitude towards the world. On one level, he displays a quite dismissive air, as when he says that *in* the world 'no value exists – and if it did exist, it would have no value' (TLP 6.41). Although this coheres with his stress on 'what is higher', it does not resonate with the typical pantheistic attitude, which seeks precisely to discern the divine *within* the world. Take, for example, the pantheism evident in the nature mysticism of William Wordsworth, in the poet's detection of divinity coursing through the natural world:

> . . . I have felt
> A presence that disturbs me with the joy
> Of elevated thoughts; a sense sublime
> Of something far more deeply interfused,
> Whose dwelling is the light of setting suns,
> And the round ocean and the living air,
> And the blue sky, and in the mind of man:
> A motion and a spirit, that impels
> All thinking things, all objects of all thought,
> And rolls through all things.[25]

Wordsworth would certainly have rejected the Tractarian claim that no value exists in the world, and yet there is perhaps something akin to the nature mysticism of Romantic pantheism in the pages of the *Tractatus*, something which links Wittgenstein to that great tradition, to Wordsworth, to Schleiermacher, and to Blake.

For a start, Wittgenstein's remark that our religious consciousness stems from a feeling of being dependent on something is certainly reminiscent of Schleiermacher's later account of faith as a feeling of 'absolute dependence', which he equated with 'being in relation with God'.[26] Moreover, if we turn to the earlier and more explicitly pantheistic *Speeches to the Cultured Despisers of Religion*, we also find notable points of contact. Just witness Schleiermacher's definition of religion as 'sense and taste for the Infinite',[27] resonating with the idea, found also in William Blake, that it is indeed through the world itself, through this apparently mundane world of objects, of facts, that the divine is to be found. Hence Blake's quest to discern the Infinite within the finite,

> To see a World in a Grain of Sand
> And a Heaven in a Wild Flower,
> Hold Infinity in the palm of your hand
> And Eternity in an hour.[28]

The mellifluence of the words of Blake and Wordsworth may seem far removed from the starkly ascetic structure of the *Tractatus*, and yet the same sentiment, the same stress on *feeling* as the core of religion and mysticism, can be detected even there. Wittgenstein, to recall, describes the mystical in terms of a particular feeling – the feeling *that* the world exists, and feeling it 'as a limited whole' (TLP 6.45). This is just what Blake attempted to do when looking at a grain of sand, or a flower, and the contiguity here, coupled with his *Notebook* entries identifying God with the world, is sufficient to establish Wittgenstein's rather arcane thoughts as a species of Romantic pantheism.

Another of these pantheistic remarks is worthy of our attention: 'There are two godheads: the world and my independent I' (NB 74). Wittgenstein's idea of the 'first godhead' (the world) has already been examined, but this 'second godhead' ('my independent I') seems puzzling. It is connected with the perceived *solipsism* of the early philosophy. Solipsism is the belief that only oneself exists. It is a notorious element of Wittgenstein's early thought and I will not discuss it at any length here.[29] The following comments will, however, serve to illustrate the solipsistic drift of his thoughts in the *Notebooks*.

> What has history to do with me? Mine is the first and only world!
> I want to report how *I* found the world.
> What others in the world have told me about the world is a very small and incidental part of my experience of the world.
> *I* have to judge the world, to measure things. (NB 82)

And strikingly, from the *Tractatus*:

> 6.431   So too at death the world does not alter, but comes to an end.

Why this 'I' should be considered a godhead ties in very much with Wittgenstein's pantheism. For if God is the world, and if 'I am my world' (NB 84; TLP 5.63), then by extension the 'I' is the godhead.

Such thoughts may seem bizarre, but analogous moves have previously been attempted. Consider another of Schleiermacher's descriptions of the religious *Gefühl*, in which the self merges with the universe (God):

> You lie directly on the bosom of the infinite world. In that moment, you are its soul. Through one part of your nature you feel, as your own, all its powers and its endless life.[30]

And if Wittgenstein's idea still seems idiosyncratic, then one might indicate the affinities existing between the divine 'I' of the *Notebooks* and the worldview of the Upanishads, the sacred books containing the mystical doctrines of ancient Hindu philosophy. According to the Upanishads, a person's true self is not his body, or his mind, or his character. Rather, it is *Atman*, revealed to be nothing less than *Brahman*, Absolute Reality itself. This same movement – the rejection of the apparent self, the isolation of the true self, and the identification of that true self with Absolute Reality – is encountered in Wittgenstein. The first step is made thus:

> 5.631   There is no such thing as the subject that thinks or entertains ideas.
>   If I wrote a book called *The World as I found it*, I should have to include a report on my body, and should have to say which parts were subordinate to my will, and which were not, etc., this being a method of isolating the subject, or rather of showing that in an important sense there is no subject; for it alone could *not* be mentioned in that book. –

Here Wittgenstein's argument mirrors Hume's attack on the idea of the Cartesian rational soul, based on the observation that the thinking subject cannot empirically be located.[31] For Wittgenstein, then, philosophy must dismiss as illusory the thinking self. The self with which philosophy is concerned is, rather, 'the metaphysical subject' (TLP 5.641). This metaphysical self is not found in the world: it is 'a limit of the world' (TLP 5.632), somewhat akin to our eye, which is never encountered in our visual field (cf. TLP 5.633).[32] And indeed it is nothing other than the world itself, which thus completes the connection between the true self and God: 'It is true: Man *is* the microcosm: I am my world' (NB 84).

Wittgenstein's ideas about God are undeniably intriguing, but one gains the impression that for Wittgenstein their importance stems not from their theological significance but rather from their relation to a particular way of living in the world, and that his early view of religion is *practical* rather than theoretical. And this is where the independence of the 'independent I' becomes important. The clue here is to be found in the following remarks:

> I cannot bend the happenings of the world to my will: I am completely powerless.
>
> I can only make myself independent of the world – and so in a certain sense master it – by renouncing any influence on happenings. (NB 73)

Here Wittgenstein is engaged in the oldest of philosophical enquiries: how can I find contentment in a world which is not at all conducive to my desires? His solution is simple: 'Live happily' (NB 75). One should not, however, expect happiness to mean here the pursuit of pleasure: it is no hedonistic doctrine that Wittgenstein offers. Rather, happiness is connected with 'doing the will of God', with God, of course, conceived as the world, or fate.

> In order to live happily I must be in agreement with the world. And that is what 'being happy' *means*.
>
> I am then, so to speak, in agreement with that alien will on which I appear dependent. That is to say: 'I am doing the will of God'. (NB 75)

What we are offered, then, is the precise *opposite* of hedonism: Wittgenstein's prescription for happiness is more akin to stoicism. The recipe for 'living happily' is to *accept the world* and whatever ills it may throw at us; not to rage against our sufferings and our pains, but to acquiesce in them. McGuinness contends that this is what drew Wittgenstein so passionately to the music of Schubert, for in Schubert one can encounter 'the contrast of the misery of his life and the absence of all trace of it in his music, the absence of all bitterness'.[33] So Wittgenstein's stoicism recommends both the acceptance of pointless suffering, and (crucially) the happy acceptance of death: 'Fear in face of death is the best sign of a false, i.e. a bad, life' (NB 75). Hence, if suffering, frustration, and ultimately death can be accepted by us, we will be living in agreement with the world and with fate: we will, in other words, be doing the will of God.

It is useful to note in this context just how closely Wittgenstein's religious and ethical doctrines cohere with those of Spinoza. Both begin with a characterisation of *Deus sive Natura* before prescribing what follows for life conduct as a result. In both cases this prescription is a form of stoicism. It is what Wittgenstein calls 'living happily' or 'living in agreement with the world'. Precisely the same notion emerges in the *Ethics*, where Spinoza writes that his doctrine is important inasmuch

> as it teaches us, how we ought to conduct ourselves with respect to the gifts of fortune, or matters which are not in our own power, and do not follow from our nature. For it shows us, that we should await and endure fortune's smiles or frowns with an equal mind, seeing that all things follow from the eternal decree of God.[34]

And if one prefers an Eastern link, Wittgenstein's recommendations certainly exhibit affinities with the Buddhist idea that liberation is achieved by the renunciation of desires and the abandonment of egoism.

It is by living in such a stoic fashion, living so that the world looks at you with a happy face (cf. TLP 6.43), that the seriousness and the importance of life becomes clear. Through such a life what is mystical *shows itself*. For recall: notwithstanding all his thrusting against the limits of language, Wittgenstein really wanted to say that all talk of God should be consigned to the realm of silence. But although the mystical cannot be said, it can be *shown* (cf. TLP 4.1212). It makes itself manifest (cf. TLP 6.522). One way it does this is, of course, through *action*, through a particular way of living. And it may well be that Wittgenstein's brief (and disastrous) spell as a school teacher in the 1920s was inspired by a desire to make the mystical concrete by improving the lot of the peasant children he taught.[35] It is not through such actions alone, however, that the mystical may be shown, and Engelmann has provided us with a pertinent example illustrating Wittgenstein's belief that *artistic creation* can mediate what is higher. In 1917 Engelmann sent Wittgenstein a poem by Ludwig Uhland called 'Count Eberhard's Hawthorn', which runs thus:

> Count Eberhard Rustle-Beard,
> From Württemberg's fair land,
> On holy errand steer'd
> To Palestina's strand.
>
> The while he slowly rode
> Along a woodland way;
> He cut from the hawthorn bush
> A little fresh green spray.
>
> Then in his iron helm
> The little sprig he plac'd;
> And bore it in the wars,
> And over the ocean waste.
>
> And when he reach'd his home,
> He plac'd it in the earth;
> Where little leaves and buds
> The gentle Spring call'd forth.

He went each year to it,
The Count so brave and true;
And overjoy'd was he
To witness how it grew.

The Count was worn with age
The sprig became a tree;
'Neath which the old man oft
Would sit in reverie.

The branching arch so high,
Whose whisper is so bland,
Reminds him of the past
And Palestina's strand.[36]

Wittgenstein's response to this simple poem was dramatic. Sensing that Uhland – without resorting to grand metaphysical speculation and thereby breaking the bounds of sense – had captured the significance of a life, he enthused to Engelmann that in such a manner art could *indicate* the presence of the mystical and how it touches human affairs. He wrote:

> The poem by Uhland is really magnificent. And this is how it is: if only you do not try to utter what is unutterable then *nothing* gets lost. But the unutterable will be – unutterably – *contained* in what has been uttered![37]

Here Wittgenstein's doctrine of showing what cannot be said becomes explicit. Though what is of greatest significance lies beyond sensible expression, it can none the less be intimated, so that through a person's actions, or via appropriate artistic creation, one might gain a felt sense of the meaningfulness of life. But what *is* ruled out in Wittgenstein's picture is *theology*: the presence of God could be shown to someone, but any attempt to 'babble' about God's existence must be rejected as illegitimate and nonsensical.

Engelmann has written that Wittgenstein's life and work suggests 'the possibility of a new *spiritual attitude*', an attitude summed up by the term 'wordless faith'.[38] In this faith of the future, there will be no verbal doctrines, for these become the source of misconstructions. Intimation of the divine, rather than talk of the divine, will be the heart of wordless faith. 'In the future, ideals will not be communicated by attempts to describe them, which inevitably distort, but by the models of an appropriate conduct in life.'[39] This perhaps provides the key to understanding

Wittgenstein's remark that the 'religion of the future will have to be extremely ascetic; and by that I don't mean just going without food and drink'.[40] The religion of the *Tractatus*, then, is ascetic in the sense of denying oneself the rich tapestry of doctrinal expression. In place of that, it encapsulates a stoic attitude and a particular way of looking at the world, seeing it as a 'miracle'.

In the course of this chapter we have seen how it would be a mistake to interpret Wittgenstein's early philosophy as though it were a species of positivism. Though the picture theory of meaning raises considerable problems for theologians, it was not Wittgenstein's purpose to bolster any atheistic criticism of religion. The spirit in which the *Tractatus* was written was one of profound respect both for religion and for the objects of religion: talk of God is denied for the pious reason that holiness is to be protected from linguistic distortion. Hence the affinities between Wittgenstein's early thought and that biblical theology which denies man's ability to approach the godhead. And yet the closest affinities of all exist between Wittgenstein and that generation of writers – including Schleiermacher, Wordsworth and Blake – who, inspired by 'the god-intoxicated man', Spinoza, sought to discern the Infinite within the finite, something ineffable within the humdrum world of facts. Like these thinkers, Wittgenstein's sense of an eternal reality both pervading and yet transcending the world left him deeply dissatisfied with the paltry realm of facts. Through the philosophy of the *Tractatus*, then, he tried to summon up a sense of a profounder reality, compared with which all the knowledge amassed by science, that knowledge so beloved by positivism, was as nothing. Wittgenstein's early philosophy of religion is thus no Logical Positivism. It might, rather, deserve the name of 'Logical Romanticism'.[41]

NOTES

1. For Hume's critique of religious belief, see his *Dialogues and Natural History of Religion* (Oxford: Oxford University Press, 1993). See also J. C. A. Gaskin, *Hume's Philosophy of Religion* (London: Macmillan, 1988).
2. See Ludwig Feuerbach, *The Essence of Christianity* (New York: Harper & Row, 1957), p. 200.
3. David Hume, *An Enquiry Concerning Human Understanding* (Oxford: Oxford University Press, 1975), p. 165.
4. A. J. Ayer, *Language, Truth and Logic* (Harmondsworth: Penguin, 1971), p. 50.
5. Ibid., p. 52.
6. Ibid., p. 152.
7. Wittgenstein, quoted in Paul Engelmann, *Letters from Ludwig Wittgenstein with a Memoir* (Oxford: Basil Blackwell, 1967), p. 11 (letter dated 16 January 1918).
8. Bertrand Russell, quoted in Ray Monk, *Ludwig Wittgenstein: The Duty of Genius* (London: Vintage, 1991), p. 44.

9. Wittgenstein, quoted in Monk, *Ludwig Wittgenstein*, pp. 287–8.

10. See Karl Barth, *The Epistle to the Romans* (Oxford: Oxford University Press, 1968); and Søren Kierkegaard, *Philosophical Fragments* (Princeton: Princeton University Press, 1962).

11. Engelmann, *Letters from Ludwig Wittgenstein*, p. 97.

12. Otto Neurath, quoted in A. J. Ayer, *Ludwig Wittgenstein* (Harmondsworth: Penguin, 1986), p. 32.

13. Ecclesiastes 5:2, Revised Standard Version.

14. Exodus 33:20, Revised Standard Version.

15. A phrase taken from Wittgenstein himself, having observed a crucifix above Drury's bed: 'Drury, never allow yourself to become too familiar with holy things.' M. O'C. Drury, 'Conversations with Wittgenstein', in Rhees (ed.), *Recollections of Wittgenstein* (Oxford: Oxford University Press, 1984), p.121.

16. Wittgenstein, quoted in Drury, 'Conversations with Wittgenstein', p. 107.

17. Immanuel Kant, *Critique of Pure Reason* (London: Macmillan, 1950), p. 29.

18. We are perhaps not far here from the Marquis de Sade's belief that from the standpoint of nature marital sex is no different from rape.

19. Compare Kierkegaard's words in *Philosophical Fragments*: 'The paradoxical passion of the Reason thus comes repeatedly into collision with this Unknown, which does indeed exist, but is unknown . . . What then is the Unknown? It is the limit to which the Reason repeatedly comes' (p. 55).

20. St. Augustine, *Confessions* (New York: Grosset & Dunlap, no date), Bk I Pt IV. See Wittgenstein's remarks on this passage in M. O'C. Drury, 'Some Notes on Conversations with Wittgenstein', in Rhees (ed.) *Recollections of Wittgenstein* (Oxford: Oxford University Press, 1984), pp. 89–90.

21. The so-called 'Big Typescript', from which this example is taken, was constructed by Wittgenstein in 1933. It does not, therefore, belong to the early period, but his analysis of the scapegoat ritual nevertheless illustrates well the contention that linguistic misuse is inherent in religion.

22. But see the contradictory passage in which Wittgenstein declares: 'Running against the limits of language? Language is, after all, not a cage' (VC 117).

23. John Macquarrie, *Jesus Christ in Modern Thought* (London: SCM Press, 1990), p. 106 (verse numbers added to refer to the original prologue of John's Gospel).

24. Benedict de Spinoza, quoted in R. J. Delahunty, *Spinoza* (London: Routledge & Kegan Paul, 1985), p. 125.

25. William Wordsworth, 'Lines Composed a Few Miles Above Tintern Abbey', in *Selected Poems* (London: Everyman, 1975), pp. 41–2.

26. Friedrich Schleiermacher, *The Christian Faith* (Edinburgh: T. & T. Clark, 1986), p. 12.

27. Friedrich Schleiermacher, *On Religion: Speeches to its Cultured Despisers* (New York: Harper & Row, 1958), p. 39.

28. William Blake, 'Auguries of Innocence', in *Complete Prose and Poetry of William Blake* (London: The Nonesuch Press, 1939), p. 118.

29. For a fuller analysis of the solipsism of the *Tractatus*, see Peter Hacker, *Insight and Illusion* (Oxford: Clarendon Press, 1986), pp. 81–107. For a radically different interpretation – that the *Tractatus* argues *against* solipsism – see H. O. Mounce, *Wittgenstein's Tractatus* (Oxford: Basil Blackwell, 1981), pp. 87–92.

30. Schleiermacher, *On Religion*, p. 43.

31. In order to locate the self one would have to perform a piece of introspection, and, as

Hume famously contends, this is a hopeless task: 'For my part, when I enter most intimately into what I call *myself*, I always stumble on some particular perception or other, of heat or cold, light or shade, love or hatred, pain or pleasure. I never can catch *myself* at any time without a perception, and never can observe any thing but the perception,' *A Treatise of Human Nature* (Harmondsworth: Penguin, 1984), p. 300. This failure to locate the self leads Wittgenstein to declare 'that there is no such thing as the soul' (TLP 5.5421).

32. The source of this idea was Schopenhauer, who compared the I to the 'dark point in consciousness, just as on the retina the precise point of entry of the optic nerve is blind . . . the eye sees everything except itself' (quoted in Hacker, *Insight and Illusion*, p. 88).

33. Brian McGuinness, *Wittgenstein: A Life* (London: Duckworth, 1988), p. 124.

34. Benedict de Spinoza, *The Ethics* (New York: Dover, 1955), p. 126.

35. For this interpretation of Wittgenstein's motivation in becoming a teacher, see William Warren Bartley III, *Wittgenstein* (London: Quartet, 1977), pp. 53–96.

36. Ludwig Uhland, 'Count Eberhard's Hawthorn,' translated by Alexander Platt, quoted in Engelmann, *Letters from Ludwig Wittgenstein*, pp. 83–4.

37. Wittgenstein, quoted in Engelmann, *Letters from Ludwig Wittgenstein*, p. 7 (letter dated 9 April 1917).

38. Engelmann, *Letters from Ludwig Wittgenstein*, p. 135.

39. Ibid.

40. Wittgenstein, quoted in Drury, 'Conversations with Wittgenstein,' p. 114.

41. As a final note to this chapter, it should be remarked that some commentators would take issue with my (or any) attempt to elucidate the content of Wittgenstein's thoughts on the mystical. D. Z. Phillips, for example, dismisses the idea of 'important nonsense', saying that 'when Wittgenstein said that certain views in the Tractatus lead to nonsense, he really meant it . . . While Wittgenstein said that the urge to speak nonsense should not be repressed, that was in order that we might face up to the nonsense and reflect on it, not in order that we might rest content in it' ('On Giving Practice its Due', *Religious Studies*, vol. 31, no. 1, p. 126). Such a view, I believe, distorts the spirit of the *Tractatus* and fails to recognise just how significant a hiatus there is between early Wittgenstein and positivism. Wittgenstein's own thoughts, as written to Ficker and Engelmann (and expounded above), make it clear that his consideration of the mystical represented the very heart of his early philosophy.

3

LATER THOUGHTS ON RELIGION

Just as Wittgenstein's later philosophy sought to undermine central features of the atomistic worldview, so his mature thought on religion differs markedly from that presented in the *Tractatus* and the *Notebooks*. This difference largely flows from Wittgenstein's changed view of the nature of language. From the perspective of the *Tractatus*, the sense-lessness of religious discourse was due to its inability to satisfy the criteria of meaning dictated by the picture theory, criteria which entail that the only acceptable form of language is that of the natural sciences. Language legitimately functions only when referring to (possible or actual) factual situations within the world: religion misuses language when it tries to describe what is beyond the world. We must then resist talking about what is unsayable. In the face of this Tractarian onslaught, one defence of theology might be to show how religious discourse, notwithstanding these difficulties, does function successfully to describe super-empirical realities, how it overcomes positivistic challenges to its cognitivity. But when Wittgenstein changes his mind about the nature of religious utterance it is not that kind of apologetic task that he ascribes himself.

As shown in Chapter 1, part of the purpose of Wittgenstein's later work – and principally of the *Philosophical Investigations* – is to counter his earlier contention that language functions in a uniform manner. Now conceived as a family resemblance concept, language is seen to be an infinitely extendable *collection* of linguistic practices with no essence and no 'general form'. No longer given a monopoly of legitimacy, scientific discourse is just one language among many, and, as a consequence, religious discourse is not to be judged by the former's standards. The task of the later work is not to adjudicate the worth of each linguistic practice, not to rank them in value, but rather to *note the distinctive character* of each. When Wittgenstein turns his mind to matters of religion, then, his project is not that of critiquing its claim to meaningfulness. It is, rather, to elucidate the character – the specific *grammar* – of religious belief. This is achieved by careful attention to the way that religious language works in practice, a programme of enquiry exhibited in the three principal – yet fragmentary – sources for our understanding of Wittgenstein's later thought on religion: *Culture and Value*, a collection of diverse and aphoristic passages on, *inter alia*, art, music and religion; *Remarks on Frazer's Golden Bough*, which comprise thoughts on the nature of magic and primitive religion; and 'Lectures on Religious Belief', containing his thoughts on God and the Last Judgement. We will take each in turn.

3.1 CONFESSIONS OF FAITH IN *CULTURE AND VALUE*

There is something of a confessional character to Wittgenstein's early thoughts on religion. He talks in a personal manner about what he 'knows' concerning God and the meaning of life, for example. Such feelings are less present in the later work, though there are some surprising passages in *Culture and Value* which appear very much to be confessions of faith, or, at the very least, *gestures* in the direction of religious belief. Most spectacular of such thoughts is perhaps this striking meditation on the resurrection of Christ:

> What inclines even me to believe in Christ's Resurrection? It is as though I play with the thought. – If he did not rise from the dead, then he decomposed in the grave like any other man. *He is dead and decomposed*. In that case he is a teacher like any other and can no longer *help*; and once more we are orphaned and alone. So we have to content ourselves with wisdom and speculation. We are in a sort of hell where we can do nothing but dream, roofed in, as it were, and cut off from heaven. But if I am to be REALLY saved, – what I need is *certainty* – not wisdom, dreams or speculation – and this certainty is faith. And faith is faith in what is needed by my *heart*, my *soul*, not my speculative intelligence. For it is my soul with its passions, as it were with its flesh and blood, that has to be saved, not my abstract mind. (CV 33)

A number of significant points are here condensed. The first thing of note is the emphasis – encountered time and again in Wittgenstein's later thoughts on religion – that religion is a realm of *passion* rather than of intellect. Religion springs, not from the head, not from speculative enquiries, but from our emotional lives, from the passions. 'Wisdom is cold and to that extent stupid. (Faith on the other hand is a passion.)' (CV 56).[1] But what we also see in this passage is a desperate longing for salvation, coupled with the conviction that the resurrection is essential for this. This would suggest that Wittgenstein held the resurrection to be of the utmost importance, and yet at other places this emphatic statement is denied. So whereas traditional Christians would hold it crucial that Jesus, as a matter of historical fact, rose from the dead, Wittgenstein denies this.

Hence, Drury records a conversation in which he expressed to Wittgenstein his feeling that the Old Testament was no more than a collection of Hebrew folklore, the historical accuracy of which was of no significance, but that the New Testament 'lost its significance if it wasn't an account of what really happened'. Wittgenstein's response:

> For me too the Old Testament is a collection of Hebrew folklore – yes, I would use that expression. But the New Testament doesn't have to be proved to be true by historians either. It would make no difference if there had never been a historical person as Jesus is portrayed in the Gospels.[2]

Similarly, in *Culture and Value* he maintains that 'the historical accounts in the Gospels might, historically speaking, be demonstrably false and yet belief would lose nothing by this' (CV 32).[3]

Wittgenstein would not, of course, be alone in holding this to be the case. Many other thinkers have stressed the great chasm between the 'Jesus of history' (about whom little can be known) and the 'Christ of faith', the focus of Christian belief but who may have only the slightest of connections with any historical person.[4] Wittgenstein's own reason for divorcing Christianity from history is so that he can focus upon the peculiar character of religious belief. Hence:

> Christianity is not based on a historical truth; rather, it offers us a (historical) narrative and says: now believe! But not, believe this narrative with the belief appropriate to a historical narrative, rather: believe, through thick and thin, which you can do only as the result of a life. *Here you have a narrative, don't take the same attitude to it as you take to other historical narratives!* Make a *quite different* place in your life for it. (CV 32)

Wittgenstein's fundamental point here is that a wholly different attitude is adopted by the believer to the Christian narrative than to other historical narratives. These latter will be held dispassionately and tentatively: new evidence might alter (or indeed falsify) what we had previously thought to have occurred. Contrariwise, the Christian narrative will not be held tentatively by the believer, by that person who believes 'through thick and thin'. Nor indeed will it be the focus of dispassionate assent, as though one might say, 'This man Jesus was born of a virgin, and rose from the dead having removed our burden of sin; nevertheless, I am unmoved by it all.' No, the Gospel narrative will occupy a pivotal space in the believer's life, informing and regulating the life and actions of that person in a way no typical historical narrative could.

We can already detect here that Wittgenstein's mature account of religion is going to diverge quite sharply from an orthodox view. Religion is not going to be connected with any speculative beliefs, nor in any straightforward way with historical occurrences. One way we can approach Wittgenstein's alternative position is by briefly returning to his thoughts on the resurrection. Recall his striking comment that if Christ did not rise from the dead then we are 'orphaned and alone'. A prominent theme in *Culture and Value*, it appears also when Wittgenstein asks:

> What would it feel like not to have heard of Christ?
>   Should we feel left alone in the dark?
>   Do we escape such a feeling simply in the way a child escapes it when he knows there is someone in the room with him? (CV 13)

The connection here between Christ's absence and the fears of a child in a darkened room, the fears of being orphaned, may bring to mind the notion, found principally in Freud, that religion represents something like a childish state; that religious belief is the outcome of a frantic recognition that our earthly parents cannot protect us from the dangers of life; and that belief in God is thus the result of the unconscious desire to be protected, just as we were when tiny babes in our cots (recall the 'absolute safety' of the 'Lecture on Ethics'). So perhaps Wittgenstein's version of Christianity is a consciously infantile religion; a religion based not on historical enquiry nor on intellectual questing but only on wish-fulfilling fantasies.

Certainly there is a sense in which Wittgenstein sees religion as offering some sort of compensation for the ills of life. Witness:

> A man is capable of infinite torment . . ., and so too he can stand in need of infinite help.
>   The Christian religion is only for the man who needs infinite help, solely, that is, for the man who experiences infinite torment . . .
>   The Christian faith – as I see it – is a man's refuge in this *ultimate* torment. (CV 45–6)

This might remind one of Karl Marx's diagnosis of religion: in the midst of sufferings, helpless human beings take refuge in the illusions of religion, 'the heart of a heartless world'. In some instances, of course, one might well want to say that a man who did resort to religion because of the torments he experienced in life was lacking in both realism and maturity. But when Wittgenstein speaks of religion as a refuge he may have something more laudable in mind than merely the 'sigh of an oppressed creature'. His account suggests rather a *mode of orientation* in which a person perceives their life in a particular way, in a fashion comparable to the way in which the stoic adjustment of the *Notebooks* enabled an individual to 'live happily' in the world.

Though these thoughts are not elaborated in any substantial manner in *Culture and Value*, what we can extrapolate thus far is that Wittgenstein sees religion as a way of living, a way of acting, rather than a theoretical account of the world.

> I believe that one of the things Christianity says is that sound doctrines are all useless. That you have to change your *life*. (Or the *direction* of your life.) (CV 53)

One might think this plainly mistaken. After all, the history of Christianity has been one of frequent bickering and confrontation over precisely the issue of 'sound doctrines' (think about the *homoousios/homoiousios* debate, or the ramifications of the *filioque* controversy). On the other hand, Wittgenstein's contention that Christianity is essentially non-doctrinal is not intended as a comment on the history of the religion. Rather, he feels that if you penetrate to its heart, if you pay attention to its character, the prima facie impression that Christianity offers through its doctrines a theoretical account of the universe and of super-empirical realities proves to be false.

Here a word needs to be said about the method implicitly involved in this technique of showing religion to be something other than a theoretical system. It is a method used also in the *Philosophical Investigations* when Wittgenstein seeks to uncover what he sees as metaphysical confusions, and takes the form of an appeal to *usage*, characterised as the 'depth grammar' of a word or sentence:

> In the use of words one might distinguish 'surface grammar' from 'depth grammar'. What immediately impresses itself upon us about the use of a word is the way it is used in the construction of the sentence, the part of its use – one might say – that can be taken in by the ear. – And now compare the depth grammar, say of the word 'to mean', with what its surface grammar would lead us to suspect. No wonder we find it difficult to know our way about. (PI §664)

Applied to the interpretation of religion, attention to depth grammar – to the use of religious expressions – reveals that religious utterance does not function as a description of supernatural entities in a fashion analogous to science's description of *natural* entities. We saw earlier how a similar conclusion was reached regarding the apparently historical narratives of the Gospels. When we attend to the role that stories of Jesus play in the life of a believer it becomes apparent that such stories are not history, but might rather be 'rules of life . . . dressed up in pictures' (CV 29).

Some further examples of this technique will serve also to elucidate aspects of Wittgenstein's account of religion. First, one of Wittgenstein's preoccupations in *Culture and Value* is with the doctrine of predestination, the contentious idea that God chose from all eternity those who were to be saved and those who were to be damned. Wittgenstein is less than favorable towards the doctrine, feeling it to be 'ugly nonsense, irreligiousness' (CV 32). For our purposes, however, the important thing to be gleaned is Wittgenstein's thought that the dynamics of predestination, the role played by this belief in the life of the faithful, shows it to be something far less intellectual than a cool prediction of future events:

> Predestination: It is only permissible to write like this out of the most dreadful suffering – and then it means something quite different. But for the same reason it is not permissible for someone to assert it as a truth, unless he himself says it in torment. – It simply isn't a theory. – Or, to put it another way: If this is truth, it is not the truth that seems at first sight to be expressed by these words. It's less a theory than a sigh, or a cry. (CV 30)

So what is expressed 'at first sight' by the doctrine of predestination is a kind of hypothesis concerning the will of God, the ultimate destiny of individuals, and so on. Greater reflection, however, reveals talk of predestination to be something altogether different: an experience born of torment, and a means of adjustment to that suffering. A genuinely religious expression of predestination would then be akin to a tortured acceptance of fate.[5]

And it is not predestination alone which is revealed to be something other than a theory or a description. For Wittgenstein it is wrong to think that religious assertions, or religious questions, have a straightforwardly fact-stating or fact-demanding character:

> If someone who believes in God looks round and asks 'Where does everything I see come from?', 'Where does all this come from?', he is *not* craving for a (causal) explanation; and his question gets its point from being the expression of a certain craving. He is, namely, expressing an attitude to all explanations. (CV 85)

Traditionally, such questions have led many theologians and philosophers to attribute 'all this' to the existence of God. Proponents of the cosmological proof, such as Aquinas and Leibniz, starting from the question 'Why is there something rather than nothing?', sought to show that only by positing the existence of a deity could one understand why anything at all exists. I may, for example, be puzzled as to why I exist, and may then seek to find a reason for why I am here, appealing perhaps to the prior existence of my parents and the natural laws permitting procreation to occur. But this is not a sufficient explanation, for what of the existence of my parents, and their parents before them? And whence those laws allowing procreation? The original question can only be satisfied by the recognition that there is a God, a being whose existence is not attributable to anything else, and who stands both as the first cause of the universe and as the author of its natural laws.

Well, that argument is not indubitable.[6] But Wittgenstein's concern is not with how successfully it explains the universe. He is, rather, stressing how the original question is *not* the request for an answer. It does, indeed, *look* somewhat akin to a request for information. If I come to my desk and find there a mass of paperwork to be completed, I might demand 'Where did all this come from?', and here I will be searching for an answer, searching for someone to blame. But although the self-same words are used when the religious believer looks around the world, there is a huge difference in the *tone* of what has been uttered. And thus attention to depth grammar reveals the question to be not a demand for an answer but rather an *expression of wonder*. By extension, Wittgenstein would appear to be saying that religious doctrines and assertions should not be conceived as though they were either attempts to describe a supernatural realm or else explanations of the mundane world. Rather, they are expressive in character: predestination is a 'sigh'; talk of a creation is an expression of wonder at the beauty of the world; and so on.

It is for this reason that Wittgenstein wants to say that the exact formulation of the beliefs themselves is relatively unimportant ('sound doctrines are useless'). The emphasis now moves to the role played in a person's life by those beliefs:

> Actually I should like to say that . . . the *words* you utter or what you think as you utter them are not what matters, so much as the difference they make at various points in your life. How do I know that two people mean the same when each says he believes in God? And just the same goes for belief in the Trinity. A theology which insists on the use of *certain particular* words and phrases, and outlaws others, does not make anything clearer (Karl Barth). It gesticulates with words, as one might say, because it wants to say something and does not know how to express it. *Practice* gives the words their sense. (CV 85)

Here, then, religious expressions cease to be assessed in terms of their status as 'super-descriptions' or hypotheses with some probability of success. And the emphasis falls not on some supernatural being but on the nature of human beings themselves. The meaning of a religious expression is not its referent, but its use – in a person's life. Hence the significance of this remark:

> The way you use the word 'God' does not show *whom* you mean – but, rather, what you mean. (CV 50)

Note that Wittgenstein does not emphasise the 'what' in 'what you mean', as though the word 'God' might refer to something (only not something personal). No, we do not understand statements about God as if they were quasi-biographical statements. God is not a name, and 'God created the world' is not logically akin to 'Aneurin Bevan created the National Health Service.' The clue to understanding how religious expressions actually *do* function, is, perhaps, this remark:

> If I, who do not believe that somewhere or other there are human-superhuman beings which we might call gods – if I say 'I fear the wrath of the gods,' then this shows that with these words I can mean something or express a feeling that need not be connected with that belief. (RFGB 8)

This remark comes from Wittgenstein's *Remarks on Frazer's Golden Bough*, a set of notes which also manifest the concerns we have just discerned within *Culture and Value*; namely, the attempt to understand the distinctive character of religion and, in particular, to show that there is nothing theoretical, nothing hypothetical, about it. Indeed, it is in his comments on Frazer that Wittgenstein's later view of religious belief and practice is most clearly articulated, and to these we should now turn.

3.2 HOMOEOPATHIC MAGIC

The *Remarks on Frazer* are crucial for an understanding of Wittgenstein's account of religion, and we will have cause to return to them later. For our present purposes, the remarks are valuable inasmuch as they illustrate Wittgenstein's censure of a pervasive view of the nature of religious belief and ritual, one which sees religion as an attempt both to explain the world and to manipulate the course of nature. Wittgenstein's criticism is directed against the theories of Sir James Frazer, as presented in his masterly work *The Golden Bough*, first published in 1890. Frazer is concerned with the origin and nature of the ritual phenomena to be found in primitive cultures. Why is it, for example, that in times of severe drought members of such cultures may be seen sprinkling droplets of water on to the parched earth? Or again, what is happening when we see someone pushing pins into a small image of a hated person? *The Golden Bough* seeks answers to such questions.

Frazer's methodology is based on the idea that in order to understand why ritual actions occur we need to think ourselves into the heads of primitive ritualists and then determine what they are trying to achieve by these ceremonies. This imaginative leap results in a picture of the primitive as a helpless being in a hostile world. Untouched by science, untouched by all the advances in the understanding of the natural world that we in the civilised West have secured, the primitive finds himself lost in a world which he can neither understand nor control. And coupled with that dreadful impotence, the primitive needs to achieve certain things just to stay alive. He requires food, shelter, protection against enemies; he needs to control those natural forces which threaten his very existence. Out of necessity, then, out of the desperate need to understand his world, the primitive becomes a philosopher, and elaborates a theory of the workings of nature. This theory is *magic*.

As a theory, magic – humanity's first philosophy of life – is a system of natural law, principally consisting of two laws which describe how things in the world affect one another. The first of these laws Frazer calls the Law of Similarity (or the Law of Homoeopathy). It states, simply, that *like produces like*, or that an effect resembles its cause. The second law, the Law of Contagion (or Contiguity), asserts that *things which have once been in contact with each other continue to act on each other, even at a distance, after the physical contact has been severed*. Armed with these two laws, the primitive philosopher can begin to understand the workings of nature. And more importantly, the theory of magic grounds and makes possible a particular way of acting, and gives the primitive an opportunity to manipulate nature to his own advantage.

When the theoretical law of homoeopathy is put into practice it produces *homoeopathic magic*. Here, the magician attempts to achieve an end by imitating what is desired. So if the magician wishes to harm his enemy, he will make a small effigy of the hated person and proceed to damage or destroy it. Because 'like produces like', the injuries inflicted on the effigy will be correspondingly felt in the enemy who is so represented:

> For example, when an Ojebway Indian desires to work evil on any one, he makes a little wooden image of his enemy and runs a needle into its head or heart, or shoots an arrow into it, believing that wherever the needle pierces or the arrow strikes the image, his foe will the same instant be seized with a sharp pain in the corresponding part of his body; but if he intends to kill the person outright, he burns or buries the puppet.[7]

While such an example may serve to reinforce a perception of magic as a dark and destructive activity, it is not so that it is always used for nefarious purposes. Just as magic arises so that nature can be controlled and made advantageous to humans, so it is often applied as a benevolently utilitarian mechanism. For instance, homoeopathic magic is frequently used in an attempt to counteract the effects of a drought. Rain is made by imitation, by sprinkling water on the ground, or even by mimicking the full effects of a storm:

> In a village near Dorpat in Russia, when rain was much wanted, three men used to climb up the fir-trees of an old sacred grove. One of them drummed with a hammer

on a kettle or small cask to imitate thunder; the second knocked two fire-brands together and made the sparks fly, to imitate lightning; and the third, who was called 'the rain-maker,' had a bunch of twigs with which he sprinkled water from a vessel on all sides.[8]

Such, then, is the character of homoeopathic magic: desired events are to be produced by imitative acts.

The nature of *contagious magic* can be illustrated by the example of another method used to harm people. Here the magician gathers together either some cuttings of his enemy's hair, or nail clippings, or clothing, and burns them. These items were once in contact with the man, and their continued sympathy with him will result in his real death: as they burn so too will he be destroyed.

Though the goals aimed at by magic are perfectly reasonable, it suffers from one fatal flaw: it is absolutely futile. However many times the magician burns effigies of his foes, however much water is poured from the tops of trees, the enemies will remain and the drought continue. Magic is thus barren, an 'abortive art', a *mistake*. And of course, this mistake is ultimately detected, and with its detection the despairing sense of helplessness returns. But a new theory emerges: what controls the course of nature is not a system of laws to be bent to one's own needs, but rather certain superhuman beings – gods – to whom must be offered prayers and sacrifices as acts of appeasement and persuasion. With regard to rain-making, then, instead of imitating rain, the ritualists will resort to other methods, imploring the gods with prayer or, as in this charming example, playing on their emotions:

> In times of drought the Guanches of Teneriffe led their sheep to sacred ground, and there they separated the lambs from their dams, that their plaintive bleating might touch the heart of the god.[9]

Thus moved by the pathetic sound, divine tears would fall from the sky.

Born out of the recognised futility of magic, religion too must suffer the same fate as its predecessor. Prayers work no better than spells, and the gods are ultimately seen to be superfluous to the workings of nature. But into the space vacated by both magic and religion moves a philosophy of life which successfully explains the workings of nature, allowing human beings both to predict and to manipulate its course effectively. What has emerged is *science*, 'a golden key that opens many locks in the treasury of nature'.[10] Each of these three philosophies – magic, religion, science – has sought the same end (the explanation and manipulation of nature) but only science has proved effective. As for the adherents of magic and religion, Frazer writes that 'their errors were not wilful extravagances or the ravings of insanity, but simply hypotheses, justifiable as such at the time when they were propounded, but which a fuller experience has proved to be inadequate'.[11]

Frazer's anthropology of religion is a version of *intellectualism*, a theory characterised by two claims: first, that magic and religion arise as attempted explanations of the world; and second, that magical and religious rituals function as *instrumental* activities, by means of which ritualists attempt to achieve desired goals. Such an interpretation is not limited to an elucidation of primitive phenomena only, for in contemporary philosophy of religion Christian beliefs are also read in an intellectualist light. Theism is seen to be one (and perhaps the best) possible way of explaining the existence of the universe and/or the beauty and designedness of the world, while prayer is portrayed as efficacious in intent. Frazer would share that diagnosis, all the while seeing even the 'higher' theistic religions as essentially erroneous in character.

Wittgenstein's response to intellectualism is uncompromisingly negative, discerning in Frazer a 'narrowness of spiritual life' (RFGB 5), a narrowness which results in a total misconception of the nature of ritual:

> Frazer's account of the magical and religious notions of men is unsatisfactory: it makes these notions appear as *mistakes*.
>
> Was Augustine mistaken, then, when he called on God on every page of the *Confessions*?
>
> Well – one might say – if he was not mistaken, then the Buddhist holy-man, or some other, whose religion expresses quite different notions, surely was. But *none* of them was making a mistake except where he was putting forward a theory. (RFGB 1)

The accusation levelled against Frazer can be put in terms of surface and depth grammar. Inclined to interpret everything as a form of science, Frazer sees religious expressions of belief as constituting hypotheses or theories, and religious practices as utilitarian actions aiming at the achievement of concrete, empirical ends. Seen in such a manner, the conclusion must inevitably be that magic and religion are erroneous: ritual actions fail to influence the course of nature because their theoretical basis is radically defective. For Wittgenstein, however, this conclusion is purely a matter of presentation: 'There is a mistake only if magic is presented as science' (RFGB 4). If we move away from a surface view of ritual and attend instead to its depth grammar we will find in magic, he maintains, something other than a primitive attempt at science.

Suspicions that the intellectualist account might be faulty arise when we consider the role rituals play in a society. For Frazer this role is straightforwardly utilitarian: the rituals do for the primitive what our technological actions do for us, but while we effectively employ reliable techniques to achieve our ends, the primitive has to cope with the frustration resulting from the failures of his futile methods. Wittgenstein finds this view facile, pointing to the fact that if the primitives were as impotent as Frazer maintains they would barely survive at all. In fact, they do possess considerable skills:

> The same savage who, apparently in order to kill his enemy, sticks his knife through a picture of him, really does build his hut of wood and cuts his arrow with skill and not in effigy. (RFGB 4)

This cuts to the bone of Frazer's theory, for if Frazer is correct, we should expect to see the primitive building in effigy. The primitive would construct a miniature hut and then look about to see whether a lifesize one has magically appeared. But of course no such thing happens, and the thought then arises that magic might not be quasi-science at all; that there are perhaps two kinds of activity which we can see manifested in a culture. Hence Wittgenstein's suggestion that

> one might begin a book on anthropology in this way: When we watch the life and behaviour of men all over the earth we see that apart from what we might call animal activities, taking food &c., &c., men also carry out actions that bear a peculiar character and might be called ritualistic.
> But then it is nonsense if we go on to say that the characteristic feature of *these* actions is that they spring from wrong ideas about the physics of things. (This is what Frazer does when he says magic is really false physics, or as the case may be, false medicine, technology, &c.) (RFGB 7)

Once these two spheres of action have been separated, we can proceed to a description of magic which sees it as something other than the now-bankrupt ancestor of science.

Consider first what Wittgenstein has to say about homoeopathic magic. His criticism of the intellectualist interpretation takes the form of the simple observation that *we kiss pictures of loved ones*. This example serves two purposes. First, it links the actions of people in exotic cultures with an action commonly performed by people in the West, thus showing 'our kinship to those savages' (RFGB 10), and thereby making magic appear less alien to us. And second, it suggests a rationale for the primitive rite:

> Burning in effigy. Kissing the picture of a loved one. This is obviously *not* based on a belief that it will have a definite effect on the object which the picture represents. It aims at some satisfaction and it achieves it. Or rather, it does not *aim* at anything; we act in this way and then feel satisfied. (RFGB 4)

If I am away from the woman I love, I may carry a photograph of her with me. And when I feel the pain of her absence I may kiss that photograph, that image of her. But in kissing her image, I do not believe that she will feel the touch of my lips on her face. That kiss is simply an expression of my love. And if my love affair turns sour, if the woman hurts me, then I may tear her photograph to pieces, or burn it. But that would not be an attempt to kill her. In burning the photograph I would be expressing my anger and frustration. And there are all sorts of cases where such homoeopathic actions are performed and with no instrumental motive. During the Second World War, allied servicemen took to throwing darts at a picture of Adolf Hitler pinned to a dartboard. Yet this was no assassination attempt; it was not regarded as an easy or even possible way of winning the war. The soldiers were showing their anger, expressing their hatred for the enemy.

The implication of Wittgenstein's reflections on homoeopathic magic seems clear. If our own personal-ritual actions can be interpreted as expressive actions, might this not also be true of primitive magic? Magic in a primitive culture is not a crude form of science, and it is not simply a mistake. It is somehow expressive. The magician who crafts an image of his foe is engaged in an act, not of homicide, but of *catharsis*; an act whereby keenly-felt, sometimes hidden (and often dark) emotions are manifested. The cathartic account of ritual lays its emphasis on how we as human beings have within us certain passions, hopes and feelings which need occasionally to be let out. Ritual functions as just such an emotional safety-valve, enabling us to bring those emotions out in the open, to bring to expression our desires and wishes, both individual and collective. This theme emerges in Wittgenstein's consideration of rain-making ceremonies:

> I read, amongst many similar examples, of a rain-king in Africa to whom the people pray for rain *when the rainy season comes*. But surely this means that they do not actually think he can make rain, otherwise they would do it in the dry periods in which the land is 'a parched and arid desert'. For if we do assume that it was stupidity that once led the people to institute this office of Rain King, still they obviously knew from experience that the rains begin in March, and it would have been the Rain King's duty to perform in other periods of the year. (RFGB 12)

If it is the case that the rain-maker is consulted only when the rains are due to begin, only when the dark clouds are amassing on the horizon, and not in times of drought, then it surely makes sense to say that the intellectualist case is wrong. Instead of an attempt to bring rain, the ceremony serves as a *celebration* of the coming of rain; a celebration of the fact that the crops will not wither in the earth and die, that the streams will not dry up. And continuing the theme, Wittgenstein writes, 'towards morning, when the sun is about to rise, people celebrate rites of the coming of day, but not at night, for then they simply burn lamps' (RFGB 12). Here the idea is the same as in the rain-making example: magic serves to mark the cycles of nature, not to manipulate them.

Although this expressive interpretation of homoeopathic magic and of rain-making ceremonies does have a prima facie plausibility, it has to be said that as a general account of magic it is inadequate. Frazer, for example, documents the case of an Abyssinian king, the Alfai, who is held to be able to cast down rain, and 'if he disappoints the people's expectation and a great drought arises in the land, the Alfai is stoned to death'.[12] This suggests strongly that the ritualists do believe that the king has it within his powers to make rain, and that they are therefore not purely expressing hopes or fears. Otherwise, why would they be disappointed if he failed to make the skies open? So this is something of a stumbling block for the expressive thesis. While it does provide some effective rebuttals of gratuitous instrumentalism (placing flowers on a grave, for example, is not intended to gratify the sense of smell believed still to be possessed by the dead man), expressivism fails fully to engage with the seriousness with which ritual is undertaken in primitive society.

So there is certainly a sense in which expressivism can be said to distort the character of some ritual actions. Wittgenstein's account is, however, not straightforwardly of an expressivist nature.[13] While he does stress that primitive magic need not be instrumental in character, at times he eschews expressivism altogether, suggesting instead that ritual does indeed aim at concrete results. Just two examples:

> People at one time thought it useful to kill a man, sacrifice him to the god of fertility, in order to produce good crops. (WLA 33)

> When a man laughs too much in our company (or at least in mine), I half-involuntarily compress my lips, as if I believed I could thereby keep his closed.[14]

Such remarks, although advocating instrumentalism in these particular cases, should not be read as a capitulation to Frazer. Indeed, the second of these comments functions as a trenchant criticism of one principal contention of intellectualism, namely that rituals are dependent upon prior beliefs and are the product of reason or of thought. For Frazer, remember, magic and religion are, first and foremost, *theories*, from which ritual practices flow. Wittgenstein rejects that entirely: 'the practice does not spring from the view' (RFGB 2). No theorising is necessary before we tear to pieces pictures of those we hate, for there is something natural – something 'involuntary' – about ritual actions; actions which are not the product of thought but which spring spontaneously from human beings. Hence, in the picture-kissing example, we can let the emphasis fall, not on its apparently expressivist content, but rather on Wittgenstein's striking comment that 'we *act* in this way and then feel satisfied'. Here, it is action, not thought, that is primary. Again:

> When I am furious about something, I sometimes beat the ground or a tree with my walking-stick. But I certainly do not believe that the ground is to blame or that my beating can help anything. 'I am venting my anger'. And all rites are of this kind. Such actions my be called Instinct-actions.[15]

Wittgenstein's account of ritual is here reminiscent of R. R. Marett's striking suggestion that 'religion is something not so much thought out as danced out',[16] so that religion owes more to action than to reasoning. Indeed, Frazer's view that a person might *reason* his way to a belief in the effectiveness of effigy-burning does seem somewhat strained, in a way that the instinctual account is not. We are, before our reason is brought into play, instinctively drawn to ways of thinking which have a kind of magic about them. Hence the power of G. K. Chesterton's fairy-tale example: 'Pluck this flower and a princess will die in a castle beyond the sea'.[17] It is quite obviously false (even insane) to think that a princess' death could result from plucking a flower. And yet, just for a second, that impossibility 'seems also inevitable'.[18] Similarly, we know that burning an effigy could never harm a real person, but we may none the less instinctively and pre-rationally be drawn to an acceptance (and a fear) of the efficacy of such an act. But to repeat: such thoughts are neither reasoned nor reasonable, but are part of our disposition as human beings, and arise from what Chesterton called 'very deep things in our nature'.[19] When the question arises as to the cause of such strange and disconcerting thoughts and actions, then, Wittgenstein's answer is, quite simply, 'human life is like that' (RFGB 3).

3.3 LESSONS FROM THE LAST JUDGEMENT

The central elements of Wittgenstein's later view of religion as we find it in *Culture and Value* and in the *Remarks on Frazer* are, first, that religious belief is discontinuous with science and should not be evaluated in scientific terms. Wittgenstein's central criticism of Frazer is that he insists on presenting magic as a form of science and then condemning magic as barren because it is not successful in fulfilling the scientific task. Second, religion is not to be regarded as emerging from a rational contemplation of the world, nor does it function as a super-empirical explanation of the world. Religion is not grounded in ratiocination, but is, rather, something like a way of responding to the world, a mode of orientation, or a way of living in the world.

> It strikes me that a religious belief could only be something like a passionate commitment to a system of reference. Hence, although it's *belief*, it's really a way of living, or a way of assessing life. It's passionately seizing hold of *this* interpretation. (CV 64)

Ideas such as these are further pursued in the 'Lectures on Religious Belief', delivered in 1938. One should be aware that these are not Wittgenstein's own writings, but are, rather, notes taken by students attending his lectures. There is, however, little doubt that they accurately convey the nature of Wittgenstein's thinking on the matters addressed.

In these lectures, Wittgenstein is once again keen to explore and lay bare the distinctive grammar of religious discourse. He is concerned with the peculiarity of the ideas and language we find in religion. 'In a religious discourse we use such expressions as: "I believe that so and so will happen," and use them differently to the way in which we use them in science' (LC 57). If we think of scientific uses of language as being those in which words function as names, with sentences serving to depict facts, the discrepancy between the religious and the scientific will mean that the words and sentences used in religion will not have a straightforwardly object–naming, fact-depicting character. And indeed, this is what Wittgenstein stresses when he reflects on the meaning of 'God', seeking clarification in the manner in which this word is taught to us in our childhood.

> The word 'God' is amongst the earliest learnt – pictures and catechisms, etc. But not the same consequences as with pictures of aunts. I wasn't shown [that which the picture pictured]. (LC 59)

One may complain of a particular portrait that it has failed to capture the likeness of a person. Here one might say, 'The nose is all wrong: I barely recognise him in this picture.' But it would be bizarre if someone were to complain that an artist had failed accurately to represent the nose of God. A picture of God can in no sense be seen as a portrait. And this is not simply because, in the absence of the sitting subject, the artist has had to imagine what God looks like. (Compare: 'This is how I imagine King Arthur to have looked.') Wittgenstein says:

> Take 'God created man'. Pictures of Michelangelo showing the creation of the world. In general, there is nothing which explains the meanings of words as well as a picture, and I take it that Michelangelo was as good as anyone can be and did his best, and here is the picture of the Deity creating Adam.

> If we ever saw this, we certainly wouldn't think this the Deity. The picture has to be used in an entirely different way if we are to call the man in that queer blanket 'God', and so on . . . I could show Moore the pictures of a tropical plant. There is a technique of comparison between picture and plant. If I showed him the picture of Michelangelo and said: 'Of course, I can't show you the real thing, only the picture' . . . The absurdity is, I've never taught him the technique of using this picture. (LC 63)

When Wittgenstein thus seeks a 'technique' for employing pictures of God (and, by extension, for the word 'God' itself), the implication is that it is crucially wrong to think that 'God' is the name of some person, in the way either that 'Tony Blair' is the name of a person or that 'The Prime Minister of the United Kingdom' is the title of a person. Believing in God is not akin to believing in the Loch Ness Monster, or the Abominable Snowman.

If expressions of theistic faith (such as 'God created the world' or 'God's omniscient eye watches over all') do not function as descriptions or putative statements of fact, then what is their function? The musings in both *Culture and Value* and the *Remarks on Frazer* suggest one possibility: that talk of God is in some manner expressive of feelings, attitudes and emotions. In the 'Lectures on Religious Belief', a different (yet related) suggestion emerges, and is one we can approach by looking at Wittgenstein's thoughts on belief in the Last Judgement.

Wittgenstein's concern is with the character of such a belief and with what divides the believer and the non-believer here. On this second matter, one might be tempted to say that the difference is straightforward: one man thinks that after death he will be judged, while the other denies that such a judgement will occur. Wittgenstein, on the other hand, wants to stress that something very different is the case. The difference between the man who believes in the Last Judgement and the man who does not is not like the difference between two people, one of whom believes the Conservative Party will win the next general election and the other of whom does not.

> Suppose that someone believed in the Last Judgement, and I don't, does this mean that I believe the opposite to him, just that there won't be such a thing? I would say: 'not at all, or not always.'
>
> Suppose I say that the body will rot, and another says 'No. Particles will rejoin in a thousand years, and there will be a Resurrection of you.'
>
> If some said: 'Wittgenstein, do you believe in this?' I'd say: 'No.' 'Do you contradict the man?' I'd say: 'No.' (LC 53)

On first glance, this might appear somewhat peculiar. Surely the non-believer *does* contradict the believer. But this would be the case only if belief in a Last Judgement was some kind of bizarre prediction. And Wittgenstein is adamant that this is not so:

> Suppose, for instance, we knew people who foresaw the future; make forecasts for years and years ahead; and they described some sort of a Judgement Day. Queerly enough, even if there were such a thing, and even if it were more convincing than I have described, belief in this happening wouldn't be at all a religious belief. (LC 56)

If the belief were a prediction, then it would be quite laughable. After all, where is the evidence that such a thing will occur? A person might be converted having dreamt of such a judgement, but this would never be seen as evidence elsewhere, in science, say, or in a law court. But the fact that dreams may have an influence on a person's acceptance of religious belief arouses Wittgenstein's suspicions as to its distinctive character. The method of obtaining belief is so bizarre and the beliefs themselves so peculiar that they cannot plausibly be conceived as anything like scientific hypotheses.

> You might say: 'For a blunder, that's too big.' If you suddenly wrote numbers down on the blackboard, and then said: 'Now, I'm going to add,' and then said: '2 and 21 is 13,' etc. I'd say: 'This is no blunder.' (LC 61–2)

This might likewise apply to the phenomenon of effigy-burning, apparently in order to kill an enemy: 'For a blunder, that's too big.'

Here, then, the religious belief is seen to be something other than a belief in what, at a future date, might happen, and by the same token the theist and the atheist are not engaged in a disagreement over facts:

> Suppose someone were a believer and said: 'I believe in a Last Judgement,' and I said: 'Well, I'm not so sure. Possibly.' You would say that there is an enormous gulf between us. If he said 'There is a German aeroplane overhead,' and I said 'Possibly. I'm not so sure,' you'd say we were fairly near.
>
> It isn't a question of my being anywhere near him, but on an entirely different plane, which you could express by saying: 'You mean something altogether different, Wittgenstein.' (LC 53)

What, then, is 'altogether different' about the character of religious beliefs, and in what does the difference between believer and non-believer lie if such beliefs do not serve as descriptions of supernatural realities, or as distant predictions, or the like?

Answers to these questions are found by considering the role played in the believer's life by the idea of the Last Judgement and the attendant notion of punishment. Attention to this (psychological) function serves,

Wittgenstein maintains, to sap our instinctive feeling that the atheist must be contradicting the believer:

> Suppose you had two people, and one of them, when he had to decide which course to take, thought of retribution, and the other did not. One person might, for instance, be inclined to take everything that happened to him as a reward or punishment, and another person doesn't think of this at all.
>
> If he is ill, he may think: 'What have I done to deserve this?' This is one way of thinking of retribution. Another way is, he thinks in a general way whenever he is ashamed of himself: 'This will be punished.'
>
> Take two people, one of whom talks of his behaviour and of what happens to him in terms of retribution, the other one does not. These people think entirely differently. Yet, so far, you can't say they believe different things. (LC 54–5)

The belief in a Last Judgement, in future divine retribution, is what Wittgenstein calls a 'picture', something which is constantly before the believer's mind, entering his deliberations when he is tempted towards wrongdoing. 'Whenever he does anything, this is before his mind' (LC 53). The religious belief has, then, a central, action-determining role for the believer, 'regulating for all in his life' (LC 54).

If religious belief is described in this fashion, it would then be absurd were an atheist to reject religious belief on the grounds that the objects of religion could not be shown to exist, or that the prospect of a final reckoning was implausible. The atheist's response is entirely different from the response of the sceptic towards the occurrence of, say, extra-terrestrial abductions, where one might properly say, 'Your evidence is precarious, your witnesses unsound.' The case of the atheist runs on an entirely different track:

> Suppose someone is ill and he says: 'This is a punishment,' and I say: 'If I'm ill, I don't think of punishment at all.' If you say: 'Do you believe the opposite?' – you can call it believing the opposite, but it is entirely different from what we would normally call believing the opposite.
>
> I think differently, in a different way. I say different things to myself. I have different pictures.
>
> It is this way: if someone said: 'Wittgenstein, you don't take illness as punishment, so what do you believe?' – I'd say: 'I don't have any thoughts of punishment.' (LC 55)

Atheism is simply then the absence of religious thoughts ('I have no thoughts of God'). It is not a contradiction of belief. Just as Wittgenstein says that religions containing quite different notions do not contradict one another except where they put forward theories (cf. RFGB 1), so religion and atheism should not be understood as rival theories. They seem more like different *ways of thinking* than different *systems of thought*.

A number of significant consequences flow from the characterisation of religion as a collection of regulating pictures. For a start, understanding a religious belief now becomes a matter of appreciating how it dictates or informs the actions of the faithful. The process of understanding is not then what it is commonly taken to be: namely, understanding the nature of the apparent referents of belief, or understanding what would be the case if the belief were true. To take an example, one characteristic feature of theistic faith is the belief in divine omniscience, and there are many scriptural passages which attest to the centrality of this idea ('Thou knowest when I sit down and when I rise up'[20]). One investigation into the idea of divine omniscience might centre upon whether it is possible, or what it would mean, for a being to be all knowing, and what might flow from that state of affairs. We might uncover worrying difficulties: if an omniscient being can know all that is yet to happen, does this mean that human beings have no control over their future actions and are thus not genuinely free? For Wittgenstein, however, the pursuit of such an enquiry would be evidence of a misunderstanding of religious notions. What it means to believe in the all-seeing eye of God is to adopt a particular way of acting, or a particular mode of living, constantly hosting the thought that one's sins will ultimately be found out. The belief in divine omniscience is thus the entertainment of an admonishing picture, and to understand it is to appreciate its role in the believer's life. Understanding is emphatically not achieved via an investigation into the ontology of some metaphysical being. For Wittgenstein, such an investigation would be amusingly misplaced: 'I meant: what conclusions are you going to draw? etc. Are eyebrows going to be talked of, in connection with the Eye of God?' (LC 71). God is no Big Brother, and the exercise of divine omniscience is in no manner comparable to the activities of an ever-present and prying secret police.

The example of omniscience brings to the fore the decidedly *moral* character of religious beliefs as they are conceived by Wittgenstein. The status of the Last Judgement as a morally regulative picture – as an aid to good conduct – is clear, and Wittgenstein also lays great stress on how the word 'God' is intimately tied to morality:

> If the question arises as to the existence of a god or God, it plays an entirely different role to that of the existence of any person or object I ever heard of. One said, had to say, that one *believed* in the existence, and if one did not believe, this was regarded as something bad. Normally if I did not believe in the existence of something no one would think there was anything wrong in this. (LC 59)

If a person ceases to believe in ghosts, then those continuing to hold that such spirits do actually exist will think that person to have made a mistake about the number of beings inhabiting our world. But if someone abandons her belief in God, and leaves the church in which she formerly worshipped, those remaining in the congregation may think her, not mistaken, but *depraved*. Here, then, we really do have an

> extraordinary use of the word 'believe'. One talks of believing and at the same time one doesn't use 'believe' as one does ordinarily. You might say (in the normal use): 'You only believe – oh well . . .' Here it is used entirely differently. (LC 59–60)

The language of religion causes much perplexity because its belief-statements do not function as 'normal' beliefs, but are instead the linguistic component of a particular mode of living and cannot meaningfully be divorced from its context of conduct.

What we find in the 'Lectures on Religious Belief', then, is a moral interpretation of religion. In tune with his remark that although religion is belief, 'it is really a way of living', the contention seems to be that a religion is only apparently (only in its surface grammar) a set of quasi-theoretical statements (concerning God, the destiny of the individual, the meaning and end of history, and so on). For it is, in fact, an aid to conduct, a collection of pictures which serve to reinforce a distinctive morality, 'rules of life . . . dressed up in pictures' (CV 29).

If Wittgenstein's account of religion does run along these lines, then he can be seen to be articulating a fairly familiar style of thinking about religion, one which can (more explicitly) be seen in R. B. Braithwaite's classic paper, 'An Empiricist's View of the Nature of Religious Belief'. Braithwaite's acceptance of the verification principle entailed for him that religious discourse could not be of a cognitive nature. Instead, religious utterance serves a moral purpose, expressing and recommending a commitment to a particular way of life. Once analysed, religious statements can thus be revealed as disguised *moral* statements. So, for example, the Christian's statement that God is love is nothing other than the believer declaring 'his intention to follow an agapeistic way of life'.[21] A religion, for Braithwaite, is a collection of (fictional) stories with a psychological-cum-moral function. 'It is', he says, 'an empirical psychological fact that many people find it easier to resolve upon and to carry through a course of action which is contrary to their natural inclinations if this policy is associated in their mind with certain stories.'[22] So Christianity, for example, consists of the entertainment of certain stories – say of God creating the world, Jesus blessing children, the Sermon on the Mount, and so on – which spur the believer to good life conduct.[23]

It is easy to see where the similarities lie between Braithwaite's non-cognitive theory and Wittgenstein's later view of religion. In both instances it seems the emphasis is shifted from the apparently putatively factual nature of religious assertions on to the psychological/moral function of beliefs conceived as morally admonishing pictures. And yet to assimilate the positions of Braithwaite and Wittgenstein would result in a distortion of the latter's account. Braithwaite's view, as we have seen, is that religious pictures can entirely be reduced to ethical statements. And indeed, as the purpose of religious belief is purely to promote and bolster a particular mode of conduct, then that belief can make no claim to exclusivity: another belief or another mode of encouragement might do just as well. Such contentions would be firmly repudiated by Wittgenstein. First, he wants to say that religious expressions cannot be reduced, cannot be translated into non-religious language, cannot be given a straightforward 'cash-value'. This comes over clearly in the following exchange with Casimir Lewy, one of the students attending Wittgenstein's lectures:

> Suppose someone, before going to China, when he might never see me again, said to me: 'We might see one another after death' – would I necessarily say that I don't understand him? I might say [want to say] simply, 'Yes. I *understand* him entirely.'
>   *Lewy*: In this case, you might only mean that he expressed a certain attitude.
>   I would say 'No, it isn't the same as saying "I'm very fond of you"' – and it may not be the same as saying anything else. It says what it says. Why should you be able to substitute anything else?
>   Suppose I say: 'The man used a picture.' (LC 70–1)

So religious pictures are non-reducible. As a result, other ideas, or other expressions, cannot do just as well:

> Of certain pictures we say that they might just as well be replaced by another – e.g. we could, under certain circumstances, have one projection of an ellipse drawn instead of another.
>   [He *may* say]: 'I would have been prepared to use another picture, it would have had the same effect . . .'
>   The whole *weight* may be in the picture. (LC 71–2)

If we play a game of chess, we will (unless we are particularly finicky) care little about the exact size and shape of the chess-men we play with. One carving of a rook could do just as well as another. But in matters of religion *the whole weight may be in the picture.* Here it will make a difference if a belief changes or (over the course of time) is lost. And this is not because religious belief expresses a certain attitude towards things, nor is it that the belief is an interpretation of events (as though belief in the Last Judgement were a queer interpretation of things). On the contrary, the belief *determines* the way the believer sees the world, so much so that we can say that the believer and the non-believer inhabit *different worlds*.

This idea can be elaborated further by reference to two other aspects of Wittgenstein's thought, one from the early period and one from the later phase. Recall first the notion of 'living happily' as this emerges in the *Notebooks* and *Tractatus*. If the recommended manner of stoic acceptance is achieved, then it is not simply that the happy man reacts to the world in a manner different from that of the unhappy man. No, the effect of living happily is that

> it becomes an altogether different world. It must, so to speak, wax and wane as a whole.
> The world of the happy man is a different one from that of the unhappy man. (TLP 6.43)

In one sense, of course, the happy man and the unhappy man do *not* inhabit different worlds, for the world in which they reside is, physically, the same world. On the other hand, if someone looks at the world and sees it looking back with a happy face, then their world is very different from that of the person at whom the world scowls. Wittgenstein's point here is that being schooled in certain modes of thought and living (and indeed being schooled in religious concepts and the religious life) enables one to see a different world, to detect possibilities and patterns of meaning which would otherwise be closed to us.[24]

This brings us to the second connected aspect of Wittgenstein's thought, his celebrated discussion of 'seeing an aspect'.[25] As presented in the *Philosophical Investigations*, Wittgenstein's thoughts concern the nature of puzzle-pictures, such as the famous 'duck-rabbit':

One person may see this picture only as a rabbit, and another only as a duck. Of course, these two people *are* looking at the same picture (there is no dispute over that), but none the less there is a sense in which what each sees is different, since a duck is different from a rabbit. The point at issue is what pattern each discerns in the picture in front of them: the one person discerns a rabbit, the other a duck. Normally, a person could be brought to see both aspects of the picture, though it may be the case that someone will only be able to see it as a duck. Perhaps they have never seen a rabbit before, so that the rabbit's characteristic shape is unknown to them, or perhaps they are so held by the duck image that they fail to see anything else. The duck will not give way to the rabbit. In this case, we might speak of 'aspect-blindness', an inability to discern alternative patterns in an image. It is, Wittgenstein says, '*akin* to the lack of a "musical ear"' (PI p. 214).

The question might now arise as to whether religious belief can be understood as a species of seeing-as. Certainly we might say that the believer will see in the world patterns of meaning undetected by the atheist; she will see the world as the creation of God, will see in history a divine plan, and so on. (Think back to Wordsworth's perception of nature, how he detects 'a spirit in the woods'. Wordsworth's world is different from that of one who feels no spirit, and different possibilities emerge for each.) If religion is thus envisaged, can the atheist legitimately be accused of aspect-blindness due to his failure to see such divine patterns? Perhaps. But then the non-believer might well level the same charge against the believer, for failing to see the atheistic implications of the real suffering and absurdity characterising human life. Here we find ourselves back at the central problem of the 'Lectures on Religious Belief', namely the nature of the disagreement between believer and atheist, and in the context of 'seeing-as' this disagreement would be analogous to that of two people seeing very different things when confronted with a puzzle-picture.

Regardless of the rights and wrongs of thinking of religious belief in terms of 'seeing-as', these thoughts return us to the idea – present also in Wittgenstein's earlier philosophy of the mystical – that there is a notable connection between religion and *aesthetics*. If religious experience is somehow like aesthetic experience, for both are concerned with ways and manners of *seeing*, then it may be fruitful to think about cases of aesthetic disagreement, in order to clarify the difference between the believer and the atheist. People are often tempted to say that aesthetic disagreement consists solely of personal preferences, and Wittgenstein himself does seem to offer a contribution to that notion:

> [*Lewy*: If my landlady says a picture is lovely and I say it is hideous, we don't contradict one another.]
>   In a sense . . . you do contradict one another. She dusts it carefully, looks at it often, etc. You want to throw it in the fire . . . Suppose the landlady says: 'This is hideous', and you say: 'This is lovely' – all right, that's that. (LC 11)

If one was to say that differences in aesthetic taste were simply a matter of personal preference, of responding emotively to a particular painting or piece of music, and that religious belief was in the manner of aesthetic taste, the implication would be that the believer and the atheist simply differed in their personal views/tastes and that was all there was to it. Religion might here be described as one particular emotional response to the facts.

On the other hand, aesthetic disagreements are not generally left at satisfaction with divergent personal opinions. If someone says that the Ode to Joy is the raucous work of a musical imbecile, one who appreciates Beethoven will not leave the matter hanging there. He will try to convince the other person. He will do this, not by giving new information (as though this were a factual dispute), but by listening to the piece again, perhaps in different surroundings, pointing out and emphasising certain features.[26] We can see how this connects with the attempts one might make in order to get someone to see both aspects of the duck-rabbit picture. Thought of in this manner, there could well be legitimate attempts to alter a person's religious or non-religious view, though these would not, of course, take the form of offering intellectual 'proofs':

> Perhaps one could 'convince someone that God exists' by means of a certain kind of upbringing, by shaping his life in such and such a way. (CV 85)

It is fitting that this remark should stress just how much conversion to a religious point of view is the product of something other than intellectual engagement, for Wittgenstein's concern throughout his later thoughts on religion is with the pre-reflective, emotional roots of faith. And if it were then complained that ' "Wittgenstein is trying to undermine reason", . . . this wouldn't be false. This is actually where such questions rise' (LC 64).

Those looking for a systematic treatment of religion in the later writings of Wittgenstein will be disappointed. There is no comprehensive philosophy of religion here. What we have rather are what Iris Murdoch has fittingly called 'exasperating hints,'[27] a collection of observations and reminders about the character of religious belief and its role in the lives of the faithful. All this chapter has attempted to do is to pursue some of these thoughts and their ramifications. This will not have produced a fully coherent account of religion, but we do none the less find a unifying theme in the three sources we have considered here. This theme is that the temptation to construe religious beliefs as hypotheses, theories about metaphysical entities, the workings of the world, the ultimate destiny of history and of the individual, and so on, is fundamentally in error. This emerges clearly in Wittgenstein's savage criticisms of intellectualism, where the object of his ire is Frazer's contention that religion, like science, arises out of ratiocination, and, again like science, functions both as an attempted explanation of the course of nature and as the theoretical foundation for a mode of effective action. His alternative ideas – for example, that ritual is rooted in spontaneous emotional actions, that religion functions as a set of life-determining pictures, and that it is something like 'a passionate commitment to a system of reference' – remain indeed tantalising hints. When we turn to the works of those we may call neo-Wittgensteinian philosophers of religion, we find what is perhaps a more complete account of what Wittgenstein was hinting at.

NOTES

1. The contrast between cold wisdom and passionate faith is frequently encountered in the pages of *Culture and Value*. Hence: 'Wisdom is passionless. But faith by contrast is what Kierkegaard calls a *passion*' (CV 53); ' "Wisdom is grey." Life on the other hand and religion are full of colour' (CV 62).

2. Wittgenstein, quoted in M. O'C. Drury, 'Conversations with Wittgenstein', in Rhees (ed.), *Recollections of Wittgenstein* (Oxford: Oxford University Press, 1984), p. 101.

3. Wittgenstein proceeds to say that 'historical proof (the historical proof-game) is irrelevant to belief. This message (the Gospels) is seized on by men believingly (i.e. lovingly)' (CV 32). It is worth noting that Wittgenstein is here writing (quite self-consciously) in the spirit of Kierkegaard, whom he described as 'by far the most profound thinker of the last century' (quoted in M. O'C. Drury, 'Some Notes on Conversations with Wittgenstein', in Rhees (ed.), *Recollections of Wittgenstein* (Oxford: Oxford University Press, 1984), p. 87). Both in *Philosophical Fragments* and in *Concluding Unscientific Postscript*, Kierkegaard attempts to counter the notion that Christianity could be objectively justified, either by philosophical speculation (by, say, proving that God existed) or by historical research. Rejecting both of these, Kierkegaard claims that far from being provable (or even justifiable), Christianity by its very nature rests upon an uncertainty. Indeed, it rests on a paradox, the manifestation of the eternal in the temporal. Faced with such an absurdity, a person must simply make a *decision*, must take a 'leap' into the unknown. Such a procedure divorces religious belief from rational considerations: it becomes less of an intellectual affair and more an affair of the heart, a product of emotion, or longing.

4. On this matter, see Albert Schweitzer, *The Quest of the Historical Jesus* (London: SCM Press, 1981).

5. For discussions of Wittgenstein's thoughts on predestination, see Cyril Barrett, *Wittgenstein on Ethics and Religious Belief* (Oxford: Basil Blackwell, 1991), pp. 219–26; and Rush Rhees, 'Election and Judgement', in D. Z. Phillips (ed.), *Rush Rhees on Religion and Philosophy* (Cambridge: Cambridge University Press, 1997), pp. 238–55.

6. For criticisms of the cosmological argument, see David Hume, *Dialogues Concerning Natural Religion* (Oxford: Oxford University Press, 1993), Part IX; J. L. Mackie, *The Miracle of Theism* (Oxford: Clarendon Press, 1982), pp. 81–92; and Bertrand Russell, 'The Existence of God', in *Why I am not a Christian* (London: George Allen & Unwin, 1967), pp. 133–53.

7. J. G. Frazer, *The Golden Bough* (abridged edition) (London: Macmillan, 1922), p. 13.

8. J. G. Frazer, *The Golden Bough* (first edition) (London: Macmillan, 1890), vol. I, p. 13.

9. Ibid., pp. 19–20.

10. Frazer, *The Golden Bough* (abridged edition), p. 712.

11. Ibid., p. 264.

12. Ibid., p. 107.

13. For an argument against the expressivist interpretation of the *Remarks on Frazer's Golden Bough*, see Brian R. Clack, *Wittgenstein, Frazer and Religion* (London: Macmillan, 1999), especially pp. 21–50, 129–34.

14. Wittgenstein, 'Remarks on Frazer's Golden Bough', in C. G. Luckhardt (ed.), *Wittgenstein: Sources and Perspectives* (Hassocks: The Harvester Press, 1979), p. 73. (The version of the *Remarks on Frazer* in Luckhardt's collection contains a number of comments omitted from the Brynmill Press edition, of which the quoted remark is one.)

15. Ibid., p. 72.

16. R. R. Marett, *The Threshold of Religion* (London: Methuen, 1929), p. xxxi.

17. G. K. Chesterton, *The Everlasting Man* (London: Hodder & Stoughton, 1930), p. 121.

18. Ibid.

19. Ibid.

20. Psalms 139:2, Revised Standard Version.

21. R. B. Braithwaite, 'An Empiricist's View of the Nature of Religious Belief', in Mitchell (ed.), *The Philosophy of Religion* (Oxford: Oxford University Press, 1971), p. 81.

22. Ibid., p. 86.

23. R. G. Collingwood's theory of magic exhibits some of the same characteristics as Braithwaite's account of the function of religious stories. For Collingwood, magic is not, *pace* Frazer, the attempt to achieve some concrete end. Rather, it is conceived as a kind of dynamo that is good for the morale of the community, its rituals serving to promote and bolster solidarity and perseverance in the face of adversity. (See Collingwood, *The Principles of Art* (Oxford: Oxford University Press, 1958), pp. 57–77.)

24. In his book *God, Jesus and Belief* (Oxford: Basil Blackwell, 1984), Stewart Sutherland elaborates a comparable account of religion, maintaining that the language of theism preserves and makes possible a particular view of the world (the view *sub specie aeternitatis*), a view which cannot be attained apart from the use of that language.

25. See PI pp. 193–214.

26. See John Wisdom, 'Gods', in *Philosophy and Psychoanalysis* (Oxford: Basil Blackwell, 1953), pp. 154–61.

27. Iris Murdoch, quoted by Kai Nielsen in *An Introduction to the Philosophy of Religion* (London: Macmillan, 1982), p. 45.

4

NEO-WITTGENSTEINIAN PHILOSOPHY OF RELIGION

What has been called 'Wittgensteinian philosophy of religion' became a recognisable phenomenon even before Wittgenstein's own writings on religious belief and ritual were published and discussed. That this occurred was due to the work of a number of writers – principally Norman Malcolm, D. Z. Phillips, Rush Rhees and Peter Winch – who diligently applied the insights of Wittgenstein's later philosophy so as to illuminate the character of religion. In this chapter, I want first to outline the characteristic elements of the standard Wittgensteinian account of religion, showing how the 'language-game' and 'form of life' motifs were applied to matters of belief. Subsequent sections will document how these philosophers produced original analyses of miracles, prayer and immortality, before finally addressing the question of whether such analyses amount to a form of reductionism.

4.1 LANGUAGE-GAMES AND FIDEISM

It was in the 1950s that Rush Rhees, a close personal friend of Wittgenstein and editor of many of his works, began writing a series of striking pieces on matters of religion. These were evidently inspired by, and in many ways were a continuation of, Wittgenstein's later thoughts on the character of belief. Like Wittgenstein, Rhees is concerned to show how mistaken it is to think of religious language as a form of discourse the purpose of which is to describe 'hyper-facts'. Hence:

> 'God exists' is not a statement of fact. You might say also that it is not in the indicative mood. It is a confession – or expression – of faith. This is recognized in some way when people say that God's existence is 'necessary existence', as opposed to the 'contingency' of what exists as a matter of fact; and when they say that to doubt God's existence is a sin, as opposed to a mistake about the facts.
>
> If you ask, 'Well, when we are talking about God, does our language not *refer* to anything?', then I should want to begin, as I have tried to here, by emphasizing something of the special grammar of this language. Otherwise it is natural to think

of the way in which our physical object language may refer to something. The physical object language may refer to something. The physical object language may not refer to anything either – if someone has made a mistake, for instance, or if the language is confused. And you might think that this is what I meant if I said that the language about God does not refer to anything. Which is obviously not the point. Or you might think that I meant that the language about God was just a sort of beautiful pretence; or perhaps that it was just part of the formality of a ceremony, like after-dinner speeches. I do not mean anything of the sort, of course, and if I wanted to avoid *that* I might say that the language about God certainly does refer to something. But then I should want to say something about what it is to 'talk about God', and how different that is from talking about the moon or talking about our new house or talking about the Queen. How different the 'talking about' is, I mean. That is a difference in grammar.[1]

Here we find much that is familiar, for it is all consonant with Wittgenstein's thoughts as discussed in the previous chapter. The absolute nature of belief in God – the queer fact that it is deemed sinful not to believe in God – leads the Wittgensteinian to say that this is no simple belief in one more existent thing in the universe. Belief in God is not to be construed as the belief that there is, somewhere or other, a superhuman being who created the universe, is omnipotent, and so on. Instead, religion is intimately tied to a particular way of life, and its language is *confessional* rather than speculative. And we also find the prescription that the philosopher's task is to lay bare the peculiar grammar of religious utterance, to show its difference from the grammar of 'physical object language'.

Notwithstanding these obvious similarities, the style of philosophising about religion which is now quite habitually associated with Wittgenstein's name goes well beyond the themes we have thus far noted. And whereas Wittgenstein's thoughts were fragmentary and somewhat personal, the writings of his followers amount to a more comprehensive understanding of religious phenomena. The systematic framework for this specifically Wittgensteinian philosophy of religion was in no small part developed by Peter Winch in his book *The Idea of a Social Science*.

Winch wants to undermine the idea that the methods of the natural sciences can profitably be applied to the understanding of human and social affairs. He thus firmly opposes the view (found, for example, in John Stuart Mill's *Logic of the Moral Sciences*) 'that there can be no fundamental logical difference between the principles according to which we explain natural changes and those according to which we explain social changes'.[2] For Winch, human beings are radically unlike the non-thinking objects of scientific enquiry. To understand the life-cycle of a plant or the process of osmosis one has no need to consider anything like thoughts or motivations for action. With regard to human beings, on the other hand, understanding the actions and lifestyles of people can be successfully achieved *only* by uncovering the motivations and ideas of those people. Winch eschews, then, the seductive notion that we could have a scientific understanding of human behaviour, an understanding which, ignoring reasons and ideas, explained that behaviour by appealing to underlying mechanisms. His alternative conception stresses that understanding human behaviour 'is like applying one's knowledge of a language in order to understand a conversation rather than like applying one's knowledge of the laws of mechanics to understand the workings of a watch'.[3] A pertinent example provided by Winch concerns the social relations within a monastic community: one would be at a complete loss to understand these relations without an understanding of the religious ideas determining the monks' choice of social environment. Such ideas cannot be bypassed, but are, rather, essential.

That Winch's programme for social understanding is an application of Wittgenstein's later philosophical method should be obvious. Just as Winch replaces the scientific desire for an *explanation* of human behaviour with the *description* of the ideas underlying and informing patterns of human behaviour, so Wittgenstein consistently rejected both the idea that philosophy should take on the methods of the natural sciences, and the attendant notion that philosophy should seek to explain phenomena. Indeed, 'We must do away with all *explanation*, and description alone must take its place' (PI §109). Again: 'Philosophy simply puts everything before us, and neither explains nor deduces anything. – Since everything lies open to view there is nothing to explain' (PI §126). In Winch's hands, this injunction entails that sociology should become like philosophy (rather than biology), *laying bare* the ideas expressed in social institutions, rather than *explaining* them.

Naturally, this approach has some notable consequences for the study of religious life. Religion is to be understood, not in terms of some underlying dynamic which may be unknown or alien to the believer (witness, for example, Freudian and Durkheimian theories), but in terms of the ideas expressed *by the believers themselves*:

Consider the parable of the Pharisee and the Publican (*Luke*, 18, 9). Was the Pharisee who said 'God, I thank Thee that I am not as other men are' doing the same kind of thing as the Publican who prayed 'God be merciful unto me a sinner'? To answer this one would have to start by considering what is involved in the idea of prayer; and that is a *religious* question. In other words, the appropriate criteria for deciding whether the actions of these two men were of the same kind or not belong to religion itself.[4]

For Winch, then, it would be illegitimate to evaluate religious matters by standards or procedures alien to religion. Here we find an echo of

Wittgenstein's censure of Frazer. Just as the intellectualist must be castigated for presenting religion as an erroneous species of science, so too Vilfredo Pareto's view that the actions of a practitioner of magic are like the blunders of a businessman is to be criticised:

> Is the entrepreneur's mistake really comparable at all to the performance of a magical rite? Surely it ought rather to be compared to a *mistake* in a magical rite. The entrepreneur's mistake is a particular act . . . within the *category* of business behaviour; but magical operations themselves *constitute* a category of behaviour. Magic, in a society in which it occurs, plays a peculiar role of its own and is conducted according to considerations of its own.[5]

It is these particular contentions – that religion (or magic) constitutes a specific 'category of behaviour', and that it is 'conducted according to considerations of its own' – which, more than any other factors, characterise the neo-Wittgensteinian analysis of religion. The idea here is that, rather than there being one monolithic account of truth, meaning and rationality common to all human institutions and practices and by means of which each practice can be evaluated, there are instead an infinitely extendable number of distinctive modes of social life, each of which can be evaluated only on its own terms.

> Science is one such mode and religion is another; and each has criteria of intelligibility peculiar to itself. So within science or religion actions can be logical or illogical: in science, for example, it would be illogical to refuse to be bound by the results of a properly carried out experiment; in religion it would be illogical to suppose that one could pit one's strength against God's; and so on.[6]

What Winch calls 'modes of social life', other Wittgensteinians, culling from the *Investigations*, call 'language-games' or 'forms of life'.

To speak of religion as a language-game would be to see it as a distinctive universe of discourse, the linguistic component of a particular form of life, or way of living. Although the word 'game' has some unfortunate connotations, suggesting, perhaps, that religion is somehow lacking in seriousness, this is not an element of the designation. Rather, and as we saw in Chapter 1, Wittgenstein's introduction of the language-game analogy was intended to highlight the diverse range of linguistic phenomena, the way in which speaking is connected with particular activities, and the rule-governed nature of those activities. Each of these aspects is to the fore when religion is itself described as a language-game. First, the rules of religious discourse are found in *theology*, which 'decides what it makes sense to say to God and about God. In short, theology is the grammar of religious discourse.'[7] This idea seems to have been present in Wittgenstein's own mind, for in the *Investigations* we find him writing this:

> *Essence* is expressed by grammar.

> Grammar tells what kind of object anything is. (Theology as grammar.) (PI §§371, 373)

Here, then, the idea of theology is that of a rule-making, rule-enforcing discipline, governing what is legitimate and illegitimate to say within the language-game of religion.

In another reference to the character of theology, a reference which ties in with the second aspect of the language-game designation as stated above, Wittgenstein writes:

> How words are understood is not told by words alone. (Theology.) (Z §144)

Consistent with Wittgenstein's central idea that words without use are dead, that employment somehow inflates a word with meaning, the lesson here is that understanding a practice (in this instance, religion) cannot be achieved purely by an analysis of words and sentences. It is the activities into which those words are woven that are crucial. Recall: '*Practice* gives the words their sense' (CV 85). The characterisation of religion as a language-game is, then, meant to bring out precisely this notion: that religion is not a system of speculative thought, but is, rather, something a person *does*, a whole way of living.

The third aspect of the language-game designation serves to stress the *sui generis* character of religion and its distinctive utterance. Part of Wittgenstein's purpose in introducing the game analogy was to highlight diverse conceptions of logic, truth, rationality, and so on, by showing how these are not (in Winch's words) 'a direct gift of God',[8] but arise out of social activities in which they have their home and within which they gain their coherence and intelligibility. If this is the case, and if religion is indeed a language-game, then (at least) two things follow. First, religion cannot be understood, as it were, from without, for fully to understand religion is to engage in the religious life. Second, it will be illegitimate to criticise religion according to the standards and objectives of another language-game. The ramifications of that second consequence are quite startling. It entails, for example, that many of the great controversies of the last one hundred and fifty years have been unnecessary. For, as distinct language-games with different concerns and objectives, there should be no (theoretical) conflict between science and religion, and hence no reason why Darwin's *Origin of Species* should be seen to conflict with the creation narrative in the Book of Genesis.[9] Whereas Darwin was engaged in a scientific project to unearth the origins of human beings, Genesis only *looks* like it is doing that. In line with the character of genuinely religious discourse, it is not a (redundant) hypothesis, but has a different function, expressing, perhaps, wonder towards the grandeur and beauty of the world.

Once religion is described as a language-game, it appears to receive a certain immunity from criticism, either from the creeping encroachment of science or from atheistically-minded theorists who wish to explain it away as an illusion, a dream of the human mind, an erroneous hypothesis, or whatever. And this is not just because to do so would be to impose alien criteria on an incommensurable universe of discourse and way of life. More than that, the designation of a practice or institution as a language-game or a form of life means for the Wittgensteinian that that practice or institution is a *fait accompli*; it is a 'given' which does not admit of explanation. Says Wittgenstein:

> You must bear in mind that the language-game is so to say something unpredict-able. I mean: it is not based on grounds. It is not reasonable (or unreasonable).
>   It is there – like our life. (OC §559)

> What has to be accepted, the given, is – so one could say – *forms of life*. (PI p. 226)

> Our mistake is to look for an explanation where we ought to look at what happens as a 'proto-phenomenon'. That is, where we ought to have said: *this language-game is played*. (PI §654)

Our correct attitude to the phenomenon of religion should be to describe its characteristics, and, regardless of how bizarre it may seem, to resist the temptation to explain it away. We must 'leave everything as it is' (cf. PI §124).

All these themes are to the fore in one of D. Z. Phillips' books, significantly titled *Religion Without Explanation*. There he rejects all the usual attempts to explain away religion. Frazer is criticised on the standard Wittgensteinian grounds that he turns religion into false science; others (notably Feuerbach, Freud and Durkheim) because they have consciously failed to incorporate believers' concepts within their explana-tions. Phillips' contention is that these sceptical philosophers have all been misled by their prejudice concerning the nature of language, a prejudice which leads them to think that religious discourse is in need of explanation:

> Instead of stipulating what *must* constitute intelligible uses of language, one should look to see how language is in fact used. If one does, one comes across the use of

language found in magical and religious rites and rituals. Such language is not based on opinions or hypotheses, but is expressive . . . Faced by it, the philosopher's task is not to attempt to verify or falsify what he sees, for that makes no sense in this context. His task is a descriptive one; he gives an account of the use of language involved. He can only say that these language-games are played.[10]

It would be hard to find a more emphatic affirmation of the *fait accompli* status of religious belief. Faced with something that is 'just there', the critics' censure of religion 'makes no sense'.

No great leaps of imagination are required to see how this approach to the understanding of religion can be seen to be something of a protective strategy, a philosophical defence of religion seeking permanently to disable all sceptical attacks. For in an age in which religion has come increasingly under fire and when its most basic beliefs are widely considered erroneous, anachronistic or even meaningless, this neo-Wittgensteinian philosophy may appear to be an apologetic device which, via talk of language-games and forms of life, serves to set up an impregnable fortress around an intellectually untenable set of beliefs. This, indeed, was the earliest criticism levelled at this specific philosophy of religion, and emerged when Kai Nielsen elaborated the features of what he called 'Wittgensteinian Fideism'.

Fideism is a position adopted by some religious believers when they contend that belief rests on faith rather than on reason, and that an intellectual justification of religion is therefore unnecessary. The Wittgensteinian twist to fideism is the claim that, qua form of life, religion is a *fait accompli* which neither stands in need of justification nor should fear censure from non-religious forms of life. Nielsen highlights a number of features of this fideistic picture which he finds unacceptable. First, there is the notion that only the insider (the believer) can fully understand the nature of religion. Malcolm, for example, says of Anselm's ontological proof of the existence of God that it 'can be thoroughly understood only by one who has a view of that human "form of life" that gives rise to the idea of an infinitely great being, who views it from the *inside* not just from the outside and who has, therefore, at least some inclination to *partake* in that religious form of life'.[11] Nielsen says that while there is undoubtedly some truth in this, the Wittgensteinian contention is an absurd extension of a sound principle. Here the lesson from modern anthropological method is instructive. A deep understanding of a given tribe's culture and beliefs can be attained only by immersion in the life of that tribe and by an empathetic sharing of the tribe's perspective. On the other hand, the anthropologist does maintain an important distance from the tribe, so that his understanding of their beliefs does not (normally) extend to *adoption* of those beliefs. Why should the same not apply with regard to the religion of one's own culture, so that one could fully understand it and yet not engage in it? 'The need to start from "inside" need not preclude the recognition of clefts, inconsistencies, and elements of incoherence in the very practice (form of life).'[12] One may fully understand what is involved in the doctrine of the Trinity and yet feel this dogma to be illogical. Similar things can be said about the problem evil raises for theistic belief, the perceived irrelevance of telling things in prayer to an omniscient God, and so on.

A second of Nielsen's objections centres on what he sees as the 'compartmentalisation' of social life entailed by talking of institutions and practices as distinctive language-games. Such compartmentalisation may be plausible when considering the beliefs and practices of other cultures (the notion can be seen to emerge in Winch's account of witchcraft beliefs among the Azande and how he sees these beliefs as being immune from Western scientific evaluation[13]), but it becomes more peculiar when we consider the social life of our own culture: 'The man perplexed about God is not like the man perplexed by Azande beliefs in witchcraft substance. He is not an outsider who does not know the form of life but an insider who does.'[14]

This thought leads us to Nielsen's third criticism, namely that it is plainly mistaken to think, as the Wittgensteinian does, that because religion is a long-established *fait accompli*, its language must be in order as it is and therefore cannot be criticised or exposed as incoherent. Nielsen finds that this does not fit the facts concerning the history of religion, for

> once there was an ongoing form of life in which fairies and witches were taken to be real entities, but gradually, as we reflected on the criteria we actually use for determining whether various entities, including persons, are or are not part of the spatio-temporal world of experience, we came to give up believing in fairies and witches. That a language-game was played, that a form of life existed, did not preclude our asking about the coherence of the concepts involved and about the reality of what they conceptualised.[15]

Nielsen's charge against neo-Wittgensteinian philosophy of religion, then, is that it is a fideistic device, designed to protect religion from advancing secular criticism and which in so doing provides a distorted analysis of social institutions, one which fails to reflect our common experience of cultural life, our commonsense understanding that social practices are open to critique and can be rejected where shown to be intellectually wanting.

D. Z. Phillips, who has frequently spoken of religious beliefs as distinctive language-games, admits that to characterise religion thus can indeed lead to the kind of misgivings voiced by Nielsen, and agrees that if the Wittgensteinian account of religion did imply that kind of fideism then it certainly would be a perverse conception. Hence, in *Belief, Change and Forms of Life*, Phillips attempts to show how his account does not exhibit those factors so objectionable to Nielsen. To take the first of those, Phillips is adamant that he would never presume that only an 'insider' could understand God-talk: 'a man may see the kind of thing religious belief is and still call himself an atheist because he does not live by such beliefs'.[16] Similarly, Phillips claims that he has consistently rejected the notion of compartmentalisation, the notion that religious beliefs are logically cut off from other aspects of human life. In his work on prayer (to be considered shortly), Phillips emphasises how deeply prayer connects with the events of human life. Far from being a game-like diversion, prayer only becomes intelligible when situated in the wider flow of life, when a person feels the need to confess something, appeal for something, thank God for something, and so on. Without those deep connections to life, religion would indeed be an irrelevance.

But of course, the main source of Nielsen's stress on compartmentalisation is the suspicion, which certainly arises from a reading of Phillips' work, that the Wittgensteinian wants to protect religion from external criticism. Notwithstanding his remark that it 'makes no sense' to explain away religion, Phillips admits that there certainly are factors which can lead one to spurn religion. One such factor is the perennial problem of evil, and if religious believers 'try to explain away the reality of suffering, or try to say that all suffering has some point . . ., one may accuse them of not taking suffering seriously'.[17] Moreover, Phillips does recognise that religion rises and falls with developments within a culture, and this could not be the case were belief entirely divorced from the wider stream of social life:

> To call the belief a language-game can be misleading if it does suggest an isolated activity. Other cultural changes can affect people's worship. For example, in *Brave New World* there is a decline in the notion of moral responsibility. In such a society one can see, without too much difficulty, how the notion of God as a Judge might also be in decline.[18]

It is important to note in this context, however, that when Phillips speaks of religious belief being challenged by events or being eroded by other cultural developments, it is not the rejection of a hypothesis that he has in mind. A religious belief is not a theory which stands or falls with the evidence, but is a way of seeing the world, a way of evaluating life. So when a child's death leads to a person's apostasy, that movement is not akin to the way a falsifying experiment leads to the abandonment of a scientific hypothesis. Rather, the tragedy leaves the former believer unable to respond to the world in the way he had previously done. Perhaps he is no longer able to utter the word 'Lord', or maybe the world has for him a wretched countenance where formerly it bespoke the glory of God. With such thoughts, the charge of fideism can probably be effectively dismantled, but there may be a further reason for its dismissal. The traditional fideist is determined to defend *something* from secular attack, and as we shall see later, it may be that the Wittgensteinian account leaves religion with precious little *to* defend.

Before leaving the issue of fideism, however, one other related criticism should be voiced. This concerns the Wittgensteinians' use of the language-game and form of life concepts. Notwithstanding Malcolm's declaration that 'Religion is a form of life; it is language embedded in action – what Wittgenstein calls a "language-game",'[19] in no place does Wittgenstein himself refer to religion in such a manner. And this is not just an oversight on his part. A brief analysis of these two key terms will show why it may be ill-advised to apply them to religion.

Though Wittgenstein never attempted a definition of 'language-game', the examples he provides of these linguistic phenomena do not suggest that he had in mind anything as large as science or religion, or indeed any practice or institution whatsoever. Language-games seem, rather, to be quite small-scale units of language-usage which occur in various human contexts. Recall the list provided in the *Investigations*, which notes such examples as asking about something, greeting someone, giving orders, reporting an event, and so on (PI §23). He elsewhere speaks of the language-game with physical objects (PI p. 180) or with colours (Z §345). Obviously, such phenomena cut across the whole spectrum of social practices and are common to many varied institutions rather than being the prerogative of just one. And although Wittgenstein does speak of mathematics as a whole language-game (RFM 173), this is really the largest section of our language to receive that appellation. It has, moreover, been argued that the principal function of the language-game in Wittgenstein's later philosophy is less to designate extant social and linguistic phenomena and more to contribute to a philosophical methodology seeking to address the confusions arising from puzzlement over certain elements of language-use. Because philosophical problems emerge from a failure to see clearly the workings of language, Wittgenstein feels it helpful to *invent* simple linguistic situations which, by comparison with a troubling segment of real language, throw light on its character.[20] Whether such a heuristic interpretation exhausts the concept of a language-game is open to debate. What is not in question is the fact that there seems no textual warrant for so inflating the notion that it can be used to characterise something as large as a religion.

Much the same can be said regarding the idea of a form of life. Although what Malcolm et al. say might lead us to suspect that Wittgenstein is speaking of cultural institutions, once again Wittgenstein's own use of the concept (though vague) suggests something rather different. The term 'form of life' appears just five times in the *Investigations*, and on each occasion important clues are provided concerning the meaning of the concept:

> . . . to imagine a language means to imagine a form of life. (PI §19)

> . . . the term 'language-*game*' is meant to bring into prominence the fact that the *speaking* of language is part of an activity, or of a form of life. (PI §23)

> 'So you are saying that human agreement decides what is true and what is false?' – It is what human beings *say* that is true and false; and they agree in the *language* they use. That is not agreement in opinions but in form of life. (PI §241)

> One can imagine an animal angry, frightened, unhappy, happy, startled. But hopeful? And why not? . . .
> Can only those hope who can talk? Only those who have mastered the use of a language. That is to say, the phenomena of hope are modes of this complicated form of life. (PI p. 174)

> What has to be accepted, the given, is – so one could say – *forms of life*. (PI p. 226)

Some philosophers have chosen to interpret form of life to mean 'way of life'.[21] Such an interpretive move would open up the possibility of talking about religion as a form of life: religion would here constitute a certain mode of living. There are undoubted merits in viewing religion in such a manner. On the other hand, it is surely *not* what Wittgenstein means by a form of life. The remarks quoted above suggest, perhaps, something almost biological, something like a tendency among human beings to react in a particular fashion. Such a suggestion appears to be confirmed when Wittgenstein speaks about the role certainty plays in our lives, and how so much of our behaviour and our believing depends upon our trusting something:

> Now I would like to regard this certainty, not as something akin to hastiness or superficiality, but as a form of life.

> But that means that I want to conceive it as something that lies beyond being justified or unjustified; as it were, as something animal. (OC §§358, 359)

So a form of life is 'something animal', perhaps something typical of human beings. Hence Wittgenstein's desire to stress the naturalness of certain human reactions, such as trusting, tending, pitying.

This biological conception of a form of life certainly encapsulates much of Wittgenstein's thinking on the matter, but it does need to be qualified by a cultural addendum. It will be recalled from Chapter 1 that Wittgenstein on one occasion equated a form of life with a 'culture', and it seems that the concept of a form of life is one which balances human biology (nature, and natural tendencies and capacities) with culture (nurture, a particular kind of training).[22] Here, then, the idea seems to be that a form of life is an instinctive human way of acting, part genetic, part nurtured; biological nature refined by culture.

As a means of illuminating religious belief, this particular reading of a form of life may be of some significance (though not perhaps in the way envisaged by Malcolm), and we will return to a consideration of it in the final chapter. The language-game idea, on the other hand, seems to be misapplied when used to describe religion. Nevertheless, much of what was intended when the term was employed – the distinctive character of religious discourse, the manner in which the meaning of language is context-dependent and rooted in activity – is essential for a fruitful understanding of religious belief and practice. Once this is recognised, we can perhaps see the term 'language-game' as an unnecessary piece of jargon and allow it to slip away, concentrating instead on how the ideas it was meant to summarise enable us to grasp the nature of central aspects of religion. Indeed, Wittgensteinian philosophers of religion have been at their best when doing precisely this. We will do well, then, to turn our attention to their analyses of some of these aspects.

4.2 MIRACLES AND PRAYER

Philosophical debate concerning miracles focuses on two issues: what constitutes a miracle, and whether it is reasonable to believe that miraculous events actually occur or have historically occurred. Definitions typically reflect the commonsense impression that an event is a miraculous one when it breaks in some remarkable fashion the normal flow of things. We might think instinctively of reported healings at Lourdes, or of events related in the Bible, such as the parting of the Red Sea, the virgin birth, or Jesus raising Lazarus from the grave. In these instances, it seems as though a law of nature has been violated, and hence miracles tend to be defined in such terms. David Hume, for example, writes: 'A miracle may be accurately defined, *a transgression of a law of nature by a particular volition of the Deity or by the interposition of some invisible agent*,'[23] or, more succinctly, 'a violation of the laws of nature'.[24] Given such a definition, discussion then turns to the possibility of such events occurring and one immediately runs into Hume's challenge.

Defined as violations of natural law, miracles, according to Hume, become overwhelmingly improbable. This is because our knowledge of the laws of nature leads us to place the firmest faith in their constant functioning rather than in their flexibility. On the other hand, the source of our 'knowledge' of miracles is not our own experience of the world but rather what we have been told by other (perhaps disreputable and credulous) people. Faced with these reports, we have to decide whether it is more likely that a person reporting a miracle has been mistaken (or is trying to deceive us) or that a law of nature really has been violated. Here the answer is straightforward: it really is far less likely that the law has been transgressed. Thus we should reject stories of the miraculous. And even were we ourselves to witness an apparently miraculous event, we would be wise to draw the conclusion that our eyes have on this occasion misled us. Regardless of how vivid the event seems to be, it will be irrational to think that a law of nature has here been suspended. One might even go so far as to suggest that the very notion of 'a violation of a natural law' is incoherent. One may transgress a civil law – say, by murdering someone, or by possessing cocaine, or by breaking a speed limit – but laws of nature are not so easily flouted.

Not surprisingly, much of the philosophical literature concerning miracles has focused on whether Hume's objection to the miraculous can be refuted.[25] The Wittgensteinian contribution to the debate has focused its attention elsewhere. Applying the contextual principle of meaning, Wittgensteinian philosophers have looked to the contexts in which the exclamation 'This is a miracle' has its natural home, and have thereby sought to establish what a miracle signifies in those situations. Attention to these contexts leads to scepticism about the validity of the violation conception. Consider the now-famous example provided by R. F. Holland:

A child riding his toy motor-car strays on to an unguarded railway crossing near his house and a wheel of his car gets stuck down the side of one of the rails. An express train is due to pass with the signals in its favour and a curve in the track makes it impossible for the driver to stop his train in time to avoid any obstruction he might encounter on the crossing. The mother coming out of the house to look for her child sees him on the crossing and hears the train approaching. She runs forward shouting and waving. The little boy remains seated in his car looking downward, engrossed in the task of pedaling it free. The brakes of the train are applied and it comes to rest a few feet from the child. The mother thanks God for the miracle; which she never ceases to think of as such although, as she in due course learns, there was nothing supernatural about the manner in which the brakes of the train came to be applied. The driver had fainted, for a reason that had nothing to do with the presence of the child on the line, and the brakes were applied automatically as his hand ceased to exert pressure on the control lever. He fainted on this particular afternoon because his blood pressure had risen after an exceptionally heavy lunch during which he had quarrelled with a colleague, and the change in blood pressure caused a clot of blood to be dislodged and circulate. He fainted at the time when he did on the afternoon in question because this was the time at which the coagulation in his blood stream reached the brain.[26]

It is perfectly understandable that the boy's mother (and others) should consider this event a miracle, although it cannot without confusion be seen as divine intervention in the natural order. For Holland, this can only mean that the violation conception is too restrictive an account of miraculous events, which he instead describes as *beneficial coincidences* taken religiously.

Given this understanding of the character of miracles, it is to be expected that one and the same event could be a miracle for one person and not for another. For what constitutes a miracle is not to be decided by dispassionate reflection on the nature of a particular queer event, and the statement 'This is a miracle' is not the description of such an event, but is, rather, a description of one's *reaction* to that event, an event which may have nothing objectively puzzling about it. To think of miracles in this manner serves to place talk of the miraculous in its natural religious context, namely in the life of the believer. It is to recognise that there is no neutral use of the sentence 'It was a miracle.' To say this of an event is to signal a religious awareness of the happenings in one's life; it is a confessional statement which, perhaps, marks the change from a secular to a religious way of living.[27] What *is* inconceivable is that someone might describe an event as a miracle and then be entirely cool about it, making no place for its significance within his or her life. Once it is recognised that the miraculous is a category only intelligible within the context of religion then the violation conception becomes unworkable: if we start talking about transgressions of natural laws and whether these can occur given our understanding of physics, we have then removed the miraculous from its natural habitat and have on our hands an instance of language idling. With a Wittgensteinian analysis of the miraculous, then, the emphasis retreats from the nature of the event in itself to the perception – the response – of the witness. Given such an understanding of miracles, we can really entertain no doubts as to whether miracles do occur. The proof of the reality of miracles is that people *have* altered the direction of their lives having reacted dramatically to unexpected beneficial events (a remarkable escape from a car crash, say) or even to quotidian yet beautiful occurrences (the birth of a child, the setting of the sun).

Much of this marches with Wittgenstein's own reflections. We can here recall how in the 'Lecture on Ethics' Wittgenstein spoke of the religious view of things as being that of seeing the world as a miracle (LE 11). In his later writings, he uses the language of the miraculous in a less holistic, more piecemeal manner. Just one example:

> The miracles of nature.
>   One might say: art *shows* us the miracles of nature. It is based on the *concept* of the miracles of nature. (The blossom, just opening out. What is *marvellous* about it?) We say: 'Just look at it opening out!' (CV 56)

The importance of this remark lies once again in the emphasis it places on the reaction of the person witnessing nature's 'miracles'. One person sees the opening blossom as a miracle, while another is not so impressed, and with this difference goes a whole way of looking at, and living in, the world.

As with its treatment of the miraculous, the Wittgensteinian interpretation of prayer similarly dispenses with what could be thought of as the commonsense view. One might instinctively think that prayer is just one other case of asking someone for something, or telling someone something, with the only difference being that in this instance the person to whom one is speaking is not visibly present. For the Wittgensteinian, to think in such a manner is to be misled by surface grammar. Greater reflection on the role played by prayer in the life of the believer should lead to an awareness that the difference between 'asking something of God' and (say) 'asking something of a Member of Parliament' is not merely a difference in the methods or requests appropriate in each case. Rather, *what constitutes asking* in the religious context is different. Says Winch:

> [Prayer] cannot be elucidated by starting simply with the function 'making requests to x', substituting 'God' for 'x', and then asking what difference is made by the fact that God has different characteristics from other xs. 'Making requests of x', that is, is not a function which retains the same sense whether 'God' or some name or description of a human being is substituted for 'x'.[28]

Fully to understand the nature of prayer one has to concentrate, not on the outward form of prayer-utterance but on its employment within the context of religion.[29] This is a point constantly stressed by D. Z. Phillips in his book *The Concept of Prayer*.

One of the things that Phillips is concerned to emphasise is that, while prayer certainly makes a difference in the life of the believer, the difference is not that of God answering prayers, in the sense of bringing something about because of the believer's petition. In other words, prayer is not a means of getting things done. It is because of this that Phillips wants to draw a distinction between what we might call 'genuine' and 'superstitious' prayers. The criteria for deciding when a prayer is genuine or not are twofold. First, if genuine, the prayer must not be an aberration, unrelated to the person's life as a whole and making no difference to his future conduct. Consider:

> When men are in danger, or think they are facing death, they sometimes pray a certain kind of prayer which can be summed up as, 'O God, O God'. Bonhoeffer gives an example of this in telling of an incident during a heavy bombing raid on a concentration camp where he was a prisoner. 'As we were all lying on the floor yesterday, someone muttered "O God, O God" – he is normally a frivolous sort of chap – but I couldn't bring myself to offer him any Christian encouragement or comfort. All I did was to glance at my watch and say: "It won't last any more than ten minutes now".'[30]

The lesson drawn from this is that the 'prayers' of otherwise non-religious people are not genuine religious phenomena. Of course, if that prayerful experience of danger is followed by a change in one's life, then all very well. But 'unless prayers play a certain role in the person's life after the crisis is over, they are not characteristic of the *religious* role of prayer in the life of the believer. These prayers are far nearer superstition: kissing a rabbit's foot or touching wood.'[31]

The second criterion concerns what the prayer is expected to achieve. A prayer is superstitious if believed to be causally efficacious: in such an instance it is more of an incantation than a prayer. On Phillips' own view (which has many points of contact with Wittgenstein's treatment of homoeopathic magic), prayer is a mechanism whereby believers bring to expression concerns lying deep within them:

> When deep religious believers pray *for* something, they are not so much asking God to bring this about, but in a way telling Him of the strength of their desires. They realize that things may not go as they wish, but they are asking to be able to go on living whatever happens. In prayers of confession and in prayers of petition, the believer is trying to find a meaning and a hope that will deliver him from the elements in his life which threaten to destroy it: in the first case, his guilt, and in the second case, his desires.[32]

This might appear to be something of a therapeutic reworking of the concept of prayer. Eschewing any belief in supernatural intervention, Phillips is suggesting that the value of prayer lies in its psychological value as a technique enabling the believer to reflect on his deepest desires. Genuine prayer would here be the equivalent of revealing one's innermost secrets to a psychotherapist.

Though this may appear plausible (and may for some be compelling[33]), Phillips is not in fact offering a secularised, self-help understanding of prayer. Rather, his account fully reflects the broader elements of a Wittgensteinian account of religion, the nascent character of which we have encountered in previous chapters and which stressed a stoic acceptance of what the world throws at us, however terrible that may be. In the context of Judaism and Christianity this involves a recognition that one should surrender oneself and one's desires to the will of God. And if this is the case then the 'commonsense' view of petitionary prayer begins to look suspect, for one seems to be reversing the picture, placing oneself above God and demanding that He meet our desires. The clue, on the other hand, that genuine petitionary prayer is not a case of self-centred asking is provided by the prayer's closing words: 'Thy will be done.' If at the end of a request ('Lord, let her live') one says, 'But Thy will, not mine,' then that prayer seems nothing other than an expression of the strength of one's own desires coupled with a voiced readiness to acquiesce in the will of God. Prayer, then, is intimately connected with, and helps to effect, an acceptance of the way things are. It enables one, whatever may occur, to praise God, so that one may truly say: 'The Lord giveth and the Lord taketh away. Blessed be the name of the Lord.'

4.3 IMMORTALITY

The belief in personal immortality is central to the Christian religion, so much so indeed that St. Paul could opine that, 'If in this life only we have hope in Christ, we are of all men most miserable.'[34] The philosophical issue arising from such a belief traditionally centres on whether and how it is possible to live on after death, and (at least in the Western tradition) two principal candidates for this possibility emerge. The first of these builds upon a dualist conception of the human person, a conception found in such philosophers as Plato and Descartes. On this view, a person consists of two parts: a body and a soul (or mind). While the body is corruptible and hence subject to decay, the soul is immortal and need not therefore fear annihilation at physical death, an event which marks simply 'a freeing and separation of soul from body'.[35] Once freed from its material prison, the soul lives on, either enjoying eternal bliss in heaven or enduring the everlasting torments of hell.

Wittgenstein's rejection of dualism, noted in Chapter 1, plainly entails that, when couched in such terms, the belief in personal immortality would be unacceptable to him. We are such flesh and blood creatures that the idea of living without a body – of being purely mental beings – is either quite unintelligible or else simply unpalatable. Of course, rejection of dualism need not by itself lead to scepticism over the possibility of life after death. A notion of personhood more physicalist in character coheres perfectly well with a belief in the resurrection of the body, the second possibility for the afterlife. According to this idea, a person rises from the dead as an embodied individual or else (in Aquinas' version) their soul is rehoused in a new and glorified body. Certainly, many of the problems associated with both the feasibility and desirability of disembodied existence disappear in this rival conception, but this is not to say that it does not present difficulties of its own. Most controversy has revolved around questions of identity: if a person dies and then reappears in a resurrection world, how can we know whether the resurrected person is the same person who died or just an identical copy?[36] Wittgensteinians have tended to abstain from these controversies, though this is not to suggest agnosticism over the possibility of resurrection. Phillips just states that it is hard to believe in such a thing,[37] and if one objects that Phillips has here provided no good reasons for his disbelief, then we might say, with Rhees, 'It just seems too silly to think of looking for reasons.'[38]

Indeed, the Wittgensteinian approach to the question of immortality is characterised by the firmest of denials that a personal afterlife existence is at all a possibility. And this is due not just to insuperable difficulties in the metaphysics of post–mortem survival. Rather, an analysis of the language concerning the afterlife reveals inherent confusions and contradictions in the concept. For example, talk of an afterlife existence carries with it the notion of 'surviving death'. And that very idea is troublesome. Imagine living in a country which is engaged in a war. The enemy conducts blanket bombing raids by night which cause great devastation and loss of life. So at night you cower in fear, praying for the sun to rise and the bombs to stop falling. When the morning comes it will be perfectly natural (and intelligible) to say 'Thank God: we survived the air raid' or 'We survived another night.' And what 'survived' here means is: 'we did not die'. Now compare 'I survived the air raid' with 'I survived death.' One can, of course, imagine ironic uses of this sentence (which might then mean: 'Everyone thought I was dead, but . . .'). On the other hand, if meant seriously the sentence is contradictory, for to survive means 'not to die'. 'I survived death' therefore means 'I died and I did not die', which is patently lacking in sense.

We can see from this that the concept of an afterlife springs in part from certain confusions surrounding the meaning of death. When people talk of the afterlife it is as though death were just another event in life, something like a gateway through which we pass on our way to a higher level of existence. Such talk fails to appreciate death's finality. As W. H. Poteat has vividly made clear, my death does not constitute a change in my experience, but is the *end* of all experience for me:

'Just as Hamlet's question 'To be or not to be . . .' is logically not like 'To be or not
to be a doctor, lawyer, or merchant chief . . .', so contemplating the ending of my
life is logically not like ending a job or a marriage. It is an end of *all* possibilities for
something, namely, for what I name with the personal pronoun *I*, and not just the
ending of certain possibilities such as this or that. We can say 'After his divorce he
was remarried,' or 'he was sadder but wiser.' To go with the expression 'After he
died . . .' there are no expressions logically like 'he remarried' or 'was sadder but
wiser.'[39]

And yet to speak of a life after death is precisely to entertain such
expressions as 'After he died he was reunited with his mother,' '. . . was
happier than he had been in later life', and so on. Though such talk may
have a certain emotive function, its misrepresentation of death's nature is
serious.

It should be noted how these thoughts are consonant with what
Wittgenstein writes about death in the closing pages of the *Tractatus*.
After his words on the respective worlds of the happy and the unhappy
man, there follow these two propositions:

6.431   So too at death the world does not alter, but comes to an end.

6.4311   Death is not an event in life: we do not live to experience death.

He then broaches an issue with which the afterlife is frequently connected, namely that of the meaning of life. One constantly hears how life
gains its significance from the promise of the next world, and that without
some kind of heavenly existence our lives must be without meaning,
'waste and void'. Wittgenstein finds such talk puzzling:

6.4312   Not only is there no guarantee of the temporal immortality of the
human soul, that is to say of its eternal survival after death; but, in any
case, this assumption completely fails to accomplish the purpose for
which it has always been intended. Or is some riddle solved by my
surviving for ever? Is not this eternal life itself as much of a riddle as our
present life?

One can perhaps imagine 'awaking' from the death bed and finding oneself
in the heavenly kingdom, and yet even within this glorious paradise, *still*
thinking 'Even so, what is it all about?' Wittgenstein is not alone in
entertaining such thoughts. Heidegger, of course, saw the recognition of
death's finality to be the only way of approaching an authentic, meaningful
existence; while Bernard Williams sees the prospect of everlasting life to be
the precise opposite of the meaningfulness we desire, for it offers the
prospect of nothing other than eternal boredom.[40]

For a Wittgensteinian like Phillips, moreover, it is not just that insuperable intellectual troubles inhere in the idea of individual post-mortem survival. In addition to those worries, the notion of immortality sits uneasily with what he thinks of as genuine religiousness. If, that is, religion involves a stoic acceptance of the way things are, and if, furthermore, Christianity (as is undeniably the case) preaches a message of self-denial, then it seems most bizarre that the Christian should place such a great weight on the (self-centred) desire to continue existing for ever. It is as though the believer were here saying, 'Sure, I have denied my own wants and desires for threescore years and ten: now I want eternal compensation for all that abnegation.' Such an expectation would surely grate with the spirit of Christianity. We are left, then, with the conclusion, not just that belief in the afterlife is errant nonsense, but that it is *pernicious* errant nonsense, serving to pervert the selfless heart of Christian faith. One may consequently feel that talk of immortality should be expelled from Christianity, but Phillips contends that this is the case only with regard to a particular (and confused) account of what is meant by 'immortality of the soul'. As he stresses in *Death and Immortality*, those factors hitherto criticised – survival of death, everlasting existence of the soul – are not necessary presuppositions of the doctrine of immortality; in other words, this belief may have nothing to do with a person's continued survival after death. To defend this (perhaps counter-intuitive) thought, Phillips undertakes a careful re-examination of the characteristic religious discourse concerning eternal life.

What first needs to be undermined is the confused, yet all too common, idea that the soul is some kind of 'thing' or entity, a part of one's anatomy. The root of this confusion lies in the prejudice that a word functioning as a noun must always refer to some thing, so that just as 'hand' is the name of an object so 'soul' must be the name of a (non-physical) object. This prejudice can be dispelled by attending to the proper employment of soul-language within its natural home; namely, religious discourse. It is when our attention shifts in this direction that we realise that language concerning the soul has little to do with a metaphysical analysis of the composition of human beings and more to do with the evaluation of human conduct. When Jesus asked, 'What profiteth a man if he gain the entire world yet loseth his soul?' he was not thinking of something being lost in the way that a hat or a wallet can be lost. (Compare: 'What profiteth a man if he gain the entire world, yet loseth his legs in a skiing accident?') In this prime instance of soul-language we see clearly Phillips' point that in these contexts a man's soul 'refers to his integrity',[41] or to his moral character. Hence, if it is said of someone that he would 'sell his soul for money', this means that he has allowed himself to become materialistic, that he no longer has any deep moral sense, that he has become depraved.

The process of selling one's soul has, then, a logic radically distinct from the tragic case of an impoverished person who out of desperation resorts to selling one of her kidneys for transplantation.

Once the soul is seen no longer as a gaseous substance or a little ghost within the body, but rather as non-contingently connected with certain moral values or high traits of character, then different possibilities concerning what *immortality* of the soul might mean begin to present themselves. But first one needs to dispense with the notion that 'eternal life' is equivalent to 'endless existence', that immortality just means living for ever. Here Stewart Sutherland's analysis of the meaning of immortality's contrary – mortality – is extremely useful. The desire for immortality arises from an all too painful awareness of the limitations of a mortal existence. The question then turns to the nature of that limitation. On one level, of course, mortality is simply the fact that our existence is temporally bounded, that we are here for but a short time. The corresponding notion of immortality stresses that life continues endlessly after death. A second feeling about the limitations imposed on us by our mortal condition gives rise to a very different notion of immortality. Here mortality is encapsulated by the fear of insignificance and trivialisation, by the feeling that death might render pointless all our dreams and projects. If mortality is seen in these terms, then when we think of immortality 'we must be speaking not of a post-mortem appendage to life (not even if it is endless) but of human life as such, and of what, if anything, in human life is independent of chance and change'.[42] This changeless element is to be found in *morality*. For Phillips, moral demands, the demands of goodness, are 'eternal demands', so that 'one cannot speak of a time to be good'.[43] When we act morally, our actions take on an eternal, timeless character, which can never be rendered redundant, not even by death. If I set my sights on material acquisition or professional advancement, then what is all of that when I am dead and buried? Yet if I have been a good man, if I have tried to do what is right, then my life can never be judged ridiculous or futile, even if I die impoverished and unknown.[44] It is in such a manner that genuine moral actions, informed neither by desire nor self-interest, bear witness to 'something eternal in a man, . . . able to exist and to be grasped within every change'.[45] And truly, eternal life becomes a goal worth pursuing, and functions – in much the same way as Wittgenstein conceived the Last Judgment – as a means of evaluating how one is living, the state one's soul is in. Hence, Phillips writes:

> Eternity is not an extension of this present life, but a mode of judging it. Eternity is not *more* life, but this life seen under certain moral and religious modes of thought. This is precisely what seeing this life *sub specie aeternitatis* would amount to.[46]

Here the connection between immortality and the meaning of life suddenly becomes clear. Whereas endless duration would not be the answer to the problems of life, living in a particular way – living morally and hence eternally – is just the solution looked for.

And it is here that we can elaborate ideas concerning heaven and hell which do something other than to describe afterlife realms of reward and punishment. For the believer, heaven is to walk with God and to do His will, and that is something to be achieved in the here and now, in this life. Similarly with hell. The believer's biggest fear is to be separated from the love of God, and yet when a person commits an act of evil that action results in just such a separation, and it can then be said of that person that he is in hell, that he is damned. But that is not a prediction of where a person's soul is going, and we are not here engaged in the language of facts and hypotheses. Says Rhees:

> People have spoken of hell as being cut off from God. But to understand what this means, you have to know what despair is.
>
> So the dread of hell is . . . well, anyway, we are pretty far from theoretical belief.[47]

One final thing requiring mention here is Phillips' contention that the language of immortality must be understood in the context of overcoming death and what that entails. To overcome death is to turn away from the temporal towards the eternal, and thus eternal life is achieved by rejecting the concerns typical of temporality, specifically the instinctive concern for oneself. A person whose soul is rooted in the temporal, in the mortal, is one whose egocentric drives and desires are dominant. Such a person thinks of himself as being the very centre of the world, and it becomes for him unthinkable that death should annihilate his existence. When the religious believer turns from such temporal concerns and embraces instead eternal life, what that person has done is to reject an egocentric existence, and to undertake the self-effacing love of others. Eternal life entails therefore a dying to the self, the plainest mark of which is the relinquishing of the desire for post-mortem compensation and for everlasting survival. For the Wittgensteinian, immortality is not about the unceasing survival of the ego. It is constituted, rather, by the rejection of that very notion.

4.4 REDUCTIONISM AND RENUNCIATION

To die to the self, to live eternally, is to participate in the life of God. But here arises the question of the nature of that God. It would be a natural response were one to think that 'God' obviously refers to some very remarkable entity, an omnipotent, omniscient being who created the world and who exists independently of human beings. Phillips' version of the reality of God, on the other hand, is not of that order. God's reality is found *within* religious practices, and particularly in the act of self-denial:

> In learning by contemplation, attention, renunciation, what forgiving, thanking, loving, etc. mean in these contexts, the believer is participating in the reality of God; *this is what we mean by God's reality.*[48]

What should be clear from this is that, for the Wittgensteinian, *belief in God* is not to be understood as *belief that there is a God*.[49] Whereas belief that there is a God would be a theoretical belief, a cool belief in a putative fact (the existence of something), belief in God is more like an affective attitude. The situation is partly analogous to believing in a friend, or in the Labour Party, instances in which belief amounts to trust, or faith. In response to this, it is tempting to say that while belief in God is obviously inconceivable without attitudes of trust, awe or fear, these attitudes are only possible because the believer holds that there is a God. I have trust in my friend, but would that trust be possible if I did not also have the conviction that he exists?

Though these issues will be addressed again in the final chapter, it should here be indicated that the Wittgensteinian denial that religious attitudes must be grounded in a (more or less theoretical) belief that God exists is a product of the language-game view of religion. We are urged by Wittgenstein not to look for the foundations of language-games (so religion has no belief as its foundation), and just as games are defined by internal goals and rules, so religious discourse does not refer beyond itself to an external reality. God is contained *in the language*:

> [The religious believer is] a participant in a shared language. He must learn the use of religious concepts. What he learns is religious language; a language which he participates in along with other believers. What I am suggesting is that to know how to use this language is to know God.[50]

It is not hard to see how a passage like this has led many critics to accuse Phillips of reductionism. From being regarding as the all-powerful creator of the universe, God is reduced to little more than an important word in a language-game, something like the king in a game of chess.

The charge of reductionism can of course also be levelled against the Wittgensteinian analyses of miracles and immortality. Miracles are not divine interventions in the natural order, but ways of responding to beneficial coincidences and natural wonders. And immortality, no longer the promise of a life beyond our miserable existence here, is none other than the resigned acceptance of our mortal condition. In Phillips' hands, says John Hick, 'religious expressions are systematically deprived of the cosmic implications that they have always been assumed to have'.[51] If Hick is right, then at least the charge of fideism is false: far from defending religion from attack, the Wittgensteinian is stripping it of any substantial content. Viewed in this manner, Wittgensteinian philosophy of religion is not a protective strategy but a full capitulation to positivism. Accepting that after Hume and Ayer there can be no way of justifying the metaphysical claims made by religion, Phillips and other writers of his ilk choose, from some kind of nostalgic yearning, to preserve the *language* of religion while rejecting the objects to which that language had formerly been believed to refer.

Phillips' response to such charges is multi-faceted. First comes the claim that he is not reducing anything. This claim has sound Wittgensteinian credentials, for his specific analyses of (for example) God, prayer and immortality arise from a description of the *actual* uses of language within their natural environment. Once we pay attention to such uses it becomes clear, he says, that religious language never did have the metaphysical, 'cosmic' meaning that Hick thinks it essentially possesses. And misgivings such as those voiced by Hick tend to give rise, says Phillips, to some unfortunate counter-claims about the reality of God which distort the character of faith. Christian philosophers may want to assert that, quite apart from having a role in a language-game, God really does exist. Phillips finds such sentiments puzzling and indeed subversive of genuine religious faith, which is an absolute belief, rather than simply the belief that there just happens to be an extraordinarily powerful being at the heart of the universe. When philosophers criticise Phillips' idea of God they want to say that in order to be non-reductionistic, an account of religion must stress that God's existence is (at least believed to be) a fact. Phillips spies in such a contention an opportunity to turn the tables on his critics:

> If we mean by reductionism an attempt to reduce the significance of religious belief to something other than it is, then reductionism consists in the attempt, however sophisticated, to say that religious pictures must refer to some object; that they must describe matters of fact. That is the real reductionism which distorts the character of religious belief.[52]

Likewise, the suspicion that the Wittgensteinian account of prayer is reductionist tends to result in the elaboration of ideas of the 'efficacy of prayer', views which Phillips holds to be entirely superstitious. It is in such a manner, then, that criticism of Wittgensteinian philosophy of religion results, says Phillips, either in reductionism itself or in a perversion of religion into superstition.

Though Phillips' rejection of the reductionist label is in parts persuasive, one may none the less feel it somewhat strained to say that one who thinks that 'God' refers to a supernatural entity is reductionist. Such a person may well be misguided, but is surely not guilty of reductionism. Similarly, Phillips' use of the term 'superstition' is not without its difficulties. What he wants to say is that, in contradistinction to a 'deep' religious action, a superstition is an erroneous attempt to influence the course of events, so that superstitions 'are, as a matter of fact, blunders, mistakes, regarding causal connections'.[53] A boxer who crosses himself before a fight is superstitious if he believes that by so doing he will not come to any harm, but not so if the act is intended as a dedication of his performance; a petitionary prayer is superstitious if intended to alter the course of events, but deep if intended as a means of quelling selfish desires. The problem with introducing the concept of superstition into his discussions is twofold. First, it is impossible entirely to shake off the pejorative overtone of the term, entailing that what is meant by a superstition is simply a religious practice of which one disapproves. And second, if Phillips means by a superstition anything intended to influence the natural order of things then the unfortunate consequence is that practically everything which has formerly gone by the name of religion is in fact a 'trust in non-existent, quasi-causal connections',[54] for people really did fear the fires of hell, believed that miracles occurred, that prayer could be effective, and so on. One may well react harshly to the claim that all of that is superstitious.[55]

Moreover, some may even find the concerns placed at the heart of Phillips' account of deep religion distasteful and certainly less valuable than he himself believes. Consider once more the crucial idea of dying to the self. There is undoubtedly great importance in this idea, in the actions of serving others and (principally) in coming to a recognition of our mortal condition. Phillips' use of the writings of Simone Weil is here instructive, bringing us to see that we have no right to claim continued existence: 'We are like the beggar who said to Talleyrand: "Sir, I must live," and to whom Talleyrand replied: "I do not see the necessity for that."'[56] On the other hand, might not the ideal of dying to the self lead to a denial of all that is valuable about our lives? Consider this, from Weil's *Gravity and Grace*:

> If I thought that God sent me suffering by an act of his will and for my good, I should think that I was something, and I should miss the chief use of suffering which is to teach me that I am nothing . . .

I must love being nothing. How horrible it would be if I were something! I must love my nothingness, love being a nothingness.[57]

It just does not go without saying that such sentiments are not pathological. From the necessity of denying our self-centredness, need we really go this far? Does not this self-abasing, nothingness-seeking religion act as a confirmation of Nietzsche's suspicion that Christianity served only to destroy everything noble, everything vigorous and affirmative in human life, so that the Christian really was the 'sick animal man'?[58] With thoughts about the desirability of faith still in our minds, let us return one last time to Wittgenstein himself, and consider the repercussions of his account of religion.

NOTES

1. Rush Rhees, 'Religion and Language', in D. Z. Phillips (ed.), *Rush Rhees on Religion and Philosophy* (Cambridge: Cambridge University Press, 1997), p. 49.
2. Peter Winch, *The Idea of a Social Science* (London: Routledge & Kegan Paul, 1958), p. 71.
3. Ibid., p. 133.
4. Ibid., p. 87.
5. Ibid., p. 99.
6. Ibid., pp. 100–1.
7. D. Z. Phillips, *Faith and Philosophical Enquiry* (London: Routledge & Kegan Paul, 1970), p. 6.
8. Winch, *The Idea of a Social Science*, p. 100.
9. On this matter, see Peter Winch's paper 'Darwin, Genesis and Contradiction', in *Trying to Make Sense* (Oxford: Basil Blackwell, 1987), pp. 132–9.
10. D. Z. Phillips, *Religion Without Explanation* (Oxford: Basil Blackwell, 1976), p. 41.
11. Norman Malcolm, 'Anselm's Ontological Arguments', in *Knowledge and Certainty* (Englewood Cliffs: Prentice-Hall, 1963), p. 162.
12. Kai Nielsen, 'Wittgensteinian Fideism', *Philosophy*, vol. 42, July 1967, pp. 205–6.
13. See Peter Winch, 'Understanding a Primitive Society', in *Ethics and Action* (London: Routledge & Kegan Paul, 1972), pp. 8–49.
14. Nielsen, 'Wittgensteinian Fideism', p. 204.
15. Ibid., p. 208.
16. D. Z. Phillips, *Belief, Change and Forms of Life* (London: Macmillan, 1986), p. 12, quoting from *Religion Without Explanation*, p. 189.
17. Ibid., p. 13.
18. Ibid., pp. 15–16, quoting from *Faith and Philosophical Enquiry*, p. 120.
19. Norman Malcolm, 'The Groundlessness of Belief', in *Thought and Knowledge* (Ithaca: Cornell University Press, 1977), p. 212.
20. For this interpretation of the nature and function of language-games, see G. P. Baker and P. M. S. Hacker, *Wittgenstein: Meaning and Understanding* (Oxford: Basil Blackwell, 1984), pp. 47–56.
21. See Stewart R. Sutherland, *Atheism and the Rejection of God* (Oxford: Basil Blackwell, 1977), pp. 85–98. See also J. F. M. Hunter's treatment of the 'way of life' interpretation

(and other interpretations) in his 'Forms of Life in Wittgenstein's *Philosophical Investigations*', in E. D. Klemke (ed.), *Essays on Wittgenstein* (Chicago: University of Illinois Press, 1971), pp. 273–97.

22. See G. P. Baker & P. M. S. Hacker, *Wittgenstein: Rules, Grammar and Necessity* (Oxford: Basil Blackwell, 1985), pp. 229–51; and Brian R. Clack, *Wittgenstein, Frazer and Religion* (London: Macmillan, 1999), pp. 160–1.

23. David Hume, *An Enquiry Concerning Human Understanding* (Oxford: Clarendon Press, 1975), p. 115 (note 1).

24. Ibid., p. 114.

25. See, for example, Francis J. Beckwith, 'Hume's Evidential/Testimonial Epistemology, Probability and Miracles', in Radcliffe & White (eds), *Faith in Theory and Practice* (Chicago: Open Court, 1993), pp. 117–40; Brian Davies, *An Introduction to the Philosophy of Religion* (Oxford: Oxford University Press, 1993), pp. 190–211; Richard Swinburne, *The Concept of Miracle* (London: Macmillan, 1970).

26. R. F. Holland, 'The Miraculous', in *Against Empiricism* (Oxford: Basil Blackwell, 1980), pp. 169–70.

27. Hence Rhees' comment that 'the cash value' of the sentence 'It was the intervention of God' might be something like 'the growth of a new humility' ('Miracles', in *Rush Rhees on Religion and Philosophy*, p. 331). The Wittgensteinian, of course, would wish to shy away from any idea of giving the 'cash value' of a religious picture, for such pictures are non-translatable (recall: 'It says what it says. Why should you be able to substitute anything else?' (LC 71)).

28. Peter Winch, 'Meaning and Religious Language', in *Trying to Make Sense*, p. 119.

29. Here again we see an application of the meaning-as-use principle. Note in this context Wittgenstein's words in his lectures on aesthetics: 'If I had to say what is the main mistake made by philosophers of the present generation . . . I would say that it is that when language is looked at, what is looked at is a form of words and not the use made of the form of words' (LC 2).

30. D. Z. Phillips, *The Concept of Prayer* (London: Routledge & Kegan Paul, 1965), p. 115.

31. Ibid., p. 116.

32. Ibid., p. 121.

33. See Robert H. Thouless, *An Introduction to the Psychology of Religion* (Cambridge: Cambridge University Press, 1979), pp. 90–5, and principally his contention that the reward of petitionary prayer is 'not detailed fulfilment but the relaxation of tension which results from the conviction that the matter prayed about is left in the hands of God' (p. 92). And note Phillips' own recognition of the therapeutic value of praying (*The Concept of Prayer*, p. 121 (note 1)).

34. 1 Corinthians 15:19 (King James Version).

35. Plato, 'Phaedo', in H. Tredennick (ed.), *The Last Days of Socrates* (Harmondsworth: Penguin, 1969), p. 112.

36. See John Hick, *Death and Eternal Life* (London: Macmillan, 1985), pp. 278–96; John Hick, 'Theology and Verification', in B. Brody (ed.), *Readings in the philosophy of Religion* (Englewood Cliffs, NJ: Prentice-Hall, 1974), pp. 315–30.

37. D. Z. Phillips, *Death and Immortality* (London: Macmillan, 1970), p. 12.

38. Rush Rhees, 'Death and Immortality', in *Rush Rhees on Religion and Philosophy*, p. 211.

39. W. H. Poteat, 'Birth, Suicide and the Doctrine of Creation', in *The Primacy of Persons and the Language of Culture* (Columbia: University of Missouri Press, 1993), p. 162. See also his '"I Will Die": An Analysis', in the same volume, pp. 178–92.

40. See Martin Heidegger, *Being and Time* (Oxford: Basil Blackwell, 1962), pp. 279–311; and Bernard Williams, 'The Makropulos Case', in *Problems of the Self* (Cambridge: Cambridge University Press, 1973), pp. 82–100.

41. Phillips, *Death and Immortality*, p. 43.

42. Stewart R. Sutherland, 'What happens after death?', *Scottish Journal of Theology*, vol. 22, December 1969, p. 412.

43. Phillips, *Death and Immortality*, p. 47.

44. See Peter Winch's paper 'Can a Good Man be Harmed?', in *Ethics and Action*, pp. 193–209; and Sutherland's example of Franz Jäggerstätter as one example of a life giving witness to the eternal within human life ('What happens after death?', pp. 414–16).

45. Søren Kierkegaard, *Purity of Heart is to Will One Thing* (New York: Harper & Row, 1956), p. 36.

46. Phillips, *Death and Immortality*, p. 49.

47. Rhees, 'Death and Immortality', p. 227.

48. Phillips, *Death and Immortality*, p. 55.

49. See Norman Malcolm, 'Is it a Religious Belief that "God Exists"?', in J. Hick (ed.), *Faith and the Philosophers* (London: Macmillan, 1964), pp. 103–10; and B. R. Tilghman, *An Introduction to the Philosophy of Religion* (Oxford: Blackwell, 1994), pp. 208–18.

50. Phillips, *The Concept of Prayer*, p. 50.

51. John Hick, *Philosophy of Religion* (Englewood Cliffs: Prentice-Hall, 1983), p. 93.

52. Phillips, *Religion Without Explanation*, p. 150.

53. D. Z. Phillips, 'Primitive Reactions and the Reactions of Primitives', in *Wittgenstein and Religion* (London: Macmillan, 1993), p. 72.

54. Ibid., p. 74.

55. On Phillips' use of the concept of superstition, see Brian R. Clack, 'D. Z. Phillips, Wittgenstein and Religion', *Religious Studies*, vol. 31, March 1995, pp. 111–20; and D. Z. Phillips, 'On Giving Practice its Due – a Reply', *Religious Studies* vol. 31, March 1995, pp. 121–7.

56. Simone Weil, *Waiting on God* (London: Routledge & Kegan Paul, 1951), p. 151, quoted by Phillips in *Death and Immortality*, p. 53.

57. Simone Weil, *Gravity and Grace* (London: Routledge & Kegan Paul, 1952), p. 101.

58. Friedrich Nietzsche, *The Anti-Christ* (Harmondsworth: Penguin, 1968), p. 116.

5

AFTERMATH

5.1 SOMETHING INDECENT

M. O'C. Drury on one occasion remarked to Wittgenstein that he had been reading F. R. Tennant's *Philosophical Theology*, to which Wittgenstein responded: 'A title like that sounds to me as if it would be something indecent.'[1] What could have led Wittgenstein to say such a thing?

In part, this rather harsh judgement is a reaction to the idea that philosophy is the kind of thing that could be brought into the service of another discipline, so that theology might employ philosophy so as to refine, ground and justify the doctrines of the Christian religion. For Wittgenstein, philosophy can never be called upon to perform such an apologetic task, for its proper role is a clarificatory one. With regard to religion, the philosopher's task consists of assembling reminders of the actual usage of religious concepts within their natural home, rather than offering a theistic 'defence'. To act as such a defender of faith, as a spokesman for a religion, is thus to pervert the philosopher's calling: 'The philosopher is not a citizen of any community of ideas. That is what makes him into a philosopher' (Z §455). Moreover, philosophy is not the only victim of its marriage to theology, for the speculative disposition of the philosopher tends to lead to a misrepresentation of *religion*, which is transformed into a system of metaphysics. Hence his comment to Drury: 'The symbolism of Christianity is wonderful beyond words, but when people try to make a philosophical system out of it I find it disgusting.'[2] In the idea of philosophical theology, then, Wittgenstein saw a perversion of both philosophy and religion.

There is something else that Wittgenstein objects to, and this applies to the nature of philosophy of religion as habitually practised, regardless of whether it is undertaken in the name of faith. It is the attempt by philosophers to assess the rationality of religious belief, to seek that which would justify (or condemn) faith, that he finds particularly disagreeable. We can consider here three such ways of assessing religion. A first – dominant within the history of the philosophy of religion – focuses upon the cogency of so-called proofs of the existence of God, arguments that would be sufficient to convince a non-believer that there really was a divine being, and that religion was, as a result, rational. Wittgenstein's verdict:

> A proof of God's existence ought really to be something by means of which one could convince oneself that God exists. But I think that what *believers* who have furnished such proofs have wanted to do is give their 'belief' an intellectual analysis and foundation, although they themselves would never have come to believe as a result of such proofs. (CV 85)

The traditional arguments for the existence of God are seen, therefore, to be personal rationalisations of a belief which is itself not born of rational considerations.

A second, more recent, development within the philosophy of religion concedes that while it is true that no proof can establish with absolute certainty the existence of God, the task of the philosopher is to weigh up the evidence for and against the truth of (theistic) religion. This evidence comprises, on the one hand, such matters as the cumulative value of the theistic proofs (design, cosmological, moral, and so on), miraculous occurrences and religious experience. On the other hand, we have, say, the problem evil poses to religious belief, science's errosion of religion's plausibility, and the possibility that religion originates out of primitive humanity's feeling of helplessness. We then assess the balance of probabilities with an eye to answering this question: is theism more likely to be true than atheism? While J. L. Mackie[3] says that on balance, the evidence makes it improbable that there is a God, Richard Swinburne concludes contrariwise:

> On our total evidence theism is more probable than not . . . The experience of so many men in their moments of religious vision corroborates what nature and history shows to be quite likely – that there is a God who made and sustains man and the universe.[4]

This stress on probability is also to be found in Tennant, who, Drury told Wittgenstein, was fond of repeating Butler's aphorism, 'Probability is the guide of life.' Wittgenstein was contemptuous of that notion: 'Can you imagine St. Augustine saying that the existence of God was "highly probable"!'[5] This comment shows how Wittgenstein sees a hiatus between the religious beliefs of the faithful and the rationalistic constructions of academic philosophers. For the faithful, belief in God is no tentatively held hypothesis; it is, rather, the rock on which their entire life stands.

This is partly why one would be reluctant to say: 'These people rigorously hold the opinion (or view) that there is a Last Judgement'. 'Opinion' sounds queer.
   It is for this reason that different words are used: 'dogma', 'faith'.
   We don't talk about hypothesis, or about high probability. (LC 57)

For Wittgenstein the kind of language that informs the work of philosophers in the mould of Mackie and Swinburne is alien to the nature and spirit of religion: it is a language adopted from debates within the natural sciences, and it distorts the character of faith.

It is easy to caricature the views of philosophers of religion intent on showing that belief in God is 'quite likely', for such an approach does indeed seem somewhat at variance with the language of faith as we find it, say, in the Bible. Phillips, for example, provides a humorous translation of Psalm 139 into the probabilistic language of philosophy of religion so as to show the absurdity of thinking of faith as tentative hypothesis-holding: 'Whither shall I go from thy Spirit? or whither shall I flee from thy presence? If I ascend up into heaven, it is highly probable that thou art there: if I make my bed in hell, behold it is highly probable that thou art there also.'[6] Droll though this may be, it would however be grossly unfair to suggest that philosophers such as Swinburne and Tennant have no idea of the commitment demanded by religious belief simply because they speak of hypotheses and probability. Nor are such philosophers unaware of the unease engendered by that kind of talk. For example, Basil Mitchell – who himself sees Christian theism as an explanatory, metaphysical system requiring justification – voices precisely these concerns when he writes that religion is not primarily a theoretical matter and that the believer is not at all concerned with testing his beliefs: 'His faith is not tentative, but unconditional.'[7] Mitchell recognises that this fact poses a problem for anyone embarked on the project of justification: 'if systems of religious belief require and admit of rational justification, . . . they ought only to be accepted more or less provisionally; yet the religious believer characteristically gives whole-hearted assent to his beliefs'.[8] To defend his project, he makes a pertinent connection between systems of religious and political belief. The idea of liberal democracy, for example, enters so deeply into the activities and attitudes of the ordinary Englishman, and is so much a part of his view of the world, that it would be misleading to say that he regards it as a hypothesis. Nevertheless, it 'does not follow that liberal democracy requires no theoretical justification',[9] for one might wish to defend it against (for example) Marxist criticism.

This is not to endorse Mitchell's approach, but only to suggest that some Wittgensteinian criticisms are hasty and rhetorical. Philosophers of Mitchell's ilk are not denying the emotional nature of religious belief, nor the passionate and committed manner in which, once accepted, religious belief is held. Nevertheless, such philosophers believe that in addition to, and underlying, its affective states religious belief comprises a theory which explains the nature of the universe better than any other competing hypothesis, and that it is precisely this explanatory power which acts as its justification. From such a view follows the impossibility of any *rapprochement* between these philosophers and those influenced by Wittgenstein.

It is, indeed, the conception of explanatory justification which constitutes the third of Wittgenstein's objections to the traditional project of philosophy of religion. If religion is held to make better sense of all the evidence, then it acts as some kind of theory, and, of course, part of the purpose of Wittgenstein's *Remarks on Frazer's Golden Bough* is to counter such a notion. Religious beliefs are there presented as being less like theories and more akin to expressions of value. Furthermore, these beliefs arise in a spontaneous, non-rational way, far different from the manner in which theories are elaborated, these latter arising from a cool and patient contemplation of the world. This is partly why Wittgenstein, in the 'Lectures on Religious Belief', wants to deny that religious belief is reasonable (but nor is it unreasonable, because that 'implies rebuke'):

> I want to say: they don't treat this as a matter of reasonability.
>   Anyone who reads the Epistles will find it said: not only that it is not reasonable, but that it is folly.
>   Not only is it not reasonable, but it doesn't pretend to be. (LC 58)

The mistake made by philosophers of religion embarked on a justificatory project is that of envisaging religion as something which possesses explanatory power and which rests on intellectual foundations. According to Wittgenstein, neither of these things is the case. As we have previously seen, Wittgenstein's later conception of religion is one debarring any explanatory justification. Rather than some vast and ambitious hypothesis, religion is presented by Wittgenstein as something like a particular perspective on the world; a means of assessing life and of judging one's actions; a way of living.

In respect of this last factor, Wittgenstein begs comparison with Tolstoy. Tolstoy's influence on Wittgenstein was incalculable, and earlier we had cause to note Wittgenstein's love of *The Gospel in Brief*, a book which, he was wont to say, saved his life. Moreover, he contended that Tolstoy was one of only two European writers of recent times 'who really had something important to say about religion',[10] the other of these writers being Dostoyevsky. It would be surprising, then, were we not to find precursors of Wittgensteinian themes in the religious writings of

Tolstoy. A first such harbinger is encountered in the essay 'What is Religion and of What Does its Essence Consist?' There, Tolstoy maintains that the essence of religion lies in the establishing of 'a relation to the immediate issues of life, a relation to the entire infinite universe in time and space, conceiving of it as a whole'.[11] The connections between these words and the mystical passages of the *Tractatus* barely require identification.

An even more striking parallel can be discerned when attention is turned to Tolstoy's 'Confession', in which he tells of his return to Christianity following a period of suicidal despair in which the threat of death and the apparent meaninglessness of life were everpresent in his mind. The questions obsessing him were familiar ones: 'why do I live? Why do I wish for anything, or do anything? Or expressed another way: is there any meaning in my life that will not be annihilated by the inevitability of death which awaits me?'[12] Failing to find answers in philosophy or other speculative knowledge, Tolstoy began to look for a solution in life, and in particular, in the lives, not of sophisticated people like himself who too suffered from anxiety, but of the enormous mass of simple, uneducated people. He was no longer looking for arguments, for 'only actions showing me that they had an understanding of life that did not make them afraid, as I was, of poverty, sickness and death might have convinced me',[13] and indeed he found that the peasants worried less about death and accepted the privations of life without protest 'and with a calm and firm conviction that this is how it must be, that it cannot be otherwise and that all is for the good'.[14] The conclusion to be drawn is that the problems of life are to be solved, not by philosophical contemplation, but by living in the right way; living, that is, 'in a way that will make what is problematic disappear' (CV 27). To repeat: this is not a matter for the speculative intelligence:

> Having realized the errors in rational knowledge I found it easier to free myself from the temptation of futile theorizing. The conviction that knowledge of the truth can only be found in life stirred me to doubt the worth of my own way of life. The thing that saved me was that I managed to tear myself away from my exclusive existence and see the true life of the simple working people, and realize that this alone is genuine life. I realized that if I wanted to understand life and its meaning I had to live a genuine life and not that of a parasite.[15]

The life which Tolstoy discovered among the Russian peasantry was one in which the events of life (and death[16]) were accepted and not railed against. This could be the foundation of a religious life further augmented by the renunciation of comfort and by the Christian message of love, so that one cares little for one's own wants, focusing lovingly instead on the needs of others.

It is this notion – that Christianity consists in a manner of living which enables one to endure the sufferings of life; a manner of living characterised by love – that is uppermost in Wittgenstein's thoughts on the demands of religion:

> Christianity is not a matter of saying a lot of prayers; in fact we are told not to do that. If you and I are to live religious lives, it mustn't be that we talk a lot about religion, but that our manner of life is different. It is my belief that only if you try to be helpful to other people will you in the end find your way to God.[17]

Indeed, the whole pattern of Tolstoy's 'Confession' can be seen in Wittgenstein's life: in the abandonment of his wealth and in his ascetic lifestyle; in his desire to extricate himself from the 'parasitic' profession of philosophy, such an activity as could never answer the deepest questions of existence; and in his desire for a simple life, the life of a gardener, a monk, or a school teacher. And all of that because of the same anguish which haunted Tolstoy, the fear of a pointless and wasted life, so achingly expressed in his correspondence with Engelmann: 'I ought to have done something positive with my life, to have become a star in the sky. Instead of which I remained stuck on earth, and now I am gradually fading out.'[18]

We seem to have come some way from the description of philosophical theology as 'indecent'. But if religion is a way of life, an adjustment to the world, then its truth will have been distorted if conceived otherwise, as an explanation of the workings and purpose of the cosmos: 'If Christianity is the truth then all the philosophy that is written about it is false' (CV 83).

This theme of the failure of the philosophical–cum–theological mentality to grasp the heart of Christianity can be discerned in a tale of Tolstoy's which was among Wittgenstein's favourites. In 'The Three Hermits', a voyaging bishop is intrigued by a fisherman's tale of three holy men who live on a secluded island, praying for salvation and who have been known to aid stranded seafarers, so he instructs the captain to steer the boat towards the island. Once ashore he speaks with its three old inhabitants and is amused by their ignorance of theology and by their primitive prayer, 'Three are ye, three are we, have mercy upon us!' For a whole day the Bishop instructs the hermits in the proper way to pray, teaching them the words of the Lord's Prayer, and this with some difficulty, for the old men struggle over words which they can neither pronounce nor remember. Nevertheless, by the time night arrives, they have mastered the prayer, and the Bishop leaves the island, satisfied that his instruction has refined the hermits' religious sensibility. As he sits on the boat, however, looking back towards the island, he is disturbed by the sight of something gleaming on the water and moving very fast in the direction of the boat. Awe-struck, the Bishop sees that it is the three hermits, running upon the water as though it were dry land and beckoning the ship to stop.

> Before the ship could be stopped, the hermits had reached it, and raising their heads, all three as with one voice, began to say:
> 'We have forgotten your teaching, servant of God. As long as we kept repeating it we remembered, but when we stopped saying it for a time, a word dropped out, and now it has all gone to pieces. We can remember nothing of it. Teach us again.'
> The Bishop crossed himself, and leaning over the ship's side, said:
> 'Your own prayer will reach the Lord, men of God. It is not for me to teach you. Pray for us sinners.'[19]

The moral we may choose to extract from this tale is that it is a simple, dedicated life, rather than sophisticated doctrine and explanatory power, that constitutes genuine religion. Recall: 'one of the things Christianity says is that sound doctrines are all useless. That you have to change your *life*' (CV 53).

5.2 WITTGENSTEIN AND RADICAL THEOLOGY

In *The Will to Power* we read:

> Christianity is still possible at any time. It is not tied to any of the impudent dogmas that have adorned themselves with its name: it requires neither the doctrine of a personal God, nor that of sin, nor that of immortality, nor that of redemption, nor that of faith; it has absolutely no need of metaphysics, and even less of asceticism, even less of a Christian 'natural science.' Christianity is a *way of life*, not a system of beliefs. It tells us how to act, not what we ought to believe.[20]

One might be struck by affinities between Nietzsche's words and the account of Christianity we have seen presented by Wittgenstein. And many of our present-day radical theologians would also echo the sentiment that Christianity is still possible – and indeed preferable – after its metaphysical content has been rejected. Such theologians have elaborated what has become known as an 'anti-realist' or 'non-realist' understanding of religion, whereby religious language is not considered to refer to transcendent realities, but rather expresses human moral and spiritual ideals. It is because the idea of God can function as the focal point for human spiritual striving that Anthony Freeman can claim: 'I can still benefit from using God religiously, without believing in him as an objective and active supernatural person.'[21] The value of the religious life lies, not in the worship of (non-existent) supernatural entities, but in the specific *language* of faith, in which inhere possibilities for a fulfilling human life.

There would appear to be some obvious parallels between the non-realist understanding of faith and the account of religion offered by Wittgenstein, and it is therefore no surprise that these radical theologians have seen in him an ally in their fight against religious realism, against, that is, the view that religion is concerned with an existent deity, to which its characteristic discourse is intended to refer. In his book *The Sea of Faith*, for example, Don Cupitt reads Wittgenstein's thought on religion as pure non-realism. As with his treatment of the language of metaphysics, Wittgenstein has dragged religious discourse down from a seemingly transcendent realm and placed it firmly within the human world, so that 'faith functions as a guidance-system. It provides us with a body of images, standards for self-assessment and goals that we can use as an itinerary to find our way through life.'[22] While much of what we have hitherto considered does seem to confirm Cupitt's interpretation, we should nevertheless take a closer look at some of the central presuppositions of non-realist faith and see whether this most radical of theologies is as close to Wittgenstein's ideas as it at first sight appears.

It is first of all worth noting that Wittgenstein would forcefully deny being a 'non-realist', but not out of a desire to defend realism. On the contrary, he would see each theory as simply one side in an idling philosophical debate which takes us away from what is most crucial, namely understanding the role played by religious concepts in the lives of the faithful. Talk of either realism or non-realism removes us from the concrete situation and places us in the sterility of the seminar room. Consider some words from *Zettel* about a comparable controversy:

> One man is a convinced realist, another a convinced idealist and teaches his children accordingly. In such an important matter as the existence or non-existence of the external world they don't want to teach their children anything wrong. (Z §413)

Will the children of the idealist be taught differently? Will part of their education regarding the meaning of words like 'chair' and 'house' involve being told that these objects have no existence outside of the mind? Of course not. In which case the difference becomes only 'one of battle cry' (Z §414). Similarly, should we expect the religious education given to the children of the non-realist to vary from that given to those of the realist? The same pictures, the same texts, will be employed for both sets of children, and hence this conflict too is purely one of empty battle cries.

While this may be correct with regard to Wittgenstein's philosophical project, it would be hard to deny that more binds him to the content of the non-realist's case than to that of the realist. If the difference between the realist and the non-realist is over whether theological language refers to extra-mundane entities and events, then we can with certainty say at least this: that he is not a realist. Similarly with neo-Wittgensteinian analyses: Phillips, for example, says that 'God' is 'not the name of an individual; it does not refer to anything'.[23] It would be hard to imagine Cupitt at all disagreeing with that.

But what of other important elements of non-realist faith? Another noticeable feature is its radical anthropocentrism, whereby religion is a human creation and must therefore be the servant of human beings. The demands of autonomy lead Cupitt to a rejection of the realist understanding of God, for an objective deity would be 'spiritually oppressive'.[24] By internalising God, the believer can lose the debilitating sense of being subject to an all-powerful tyrant, and can assimilate the virtues formerly predicated of that being. The idea of immortality is similarly rejected on humanistic lines, for once we discard the poisonous idea of future happiness in a world beyond this one, we can start 'to actualize religious values in this world';[25] that is, make a heaven on earth. It is to be noted that in its thoughts on God and immortality, non-realist faith mirrors the humanism of Feuerbach, who felt both that it was necessary to reclaim those human attributes of which God was a reified projection, and that concentration on a future transcendent realm should give way to concrete social engagement in this life. The aim is

> to transform theologians into anthropologists, lovers of God into lovers of man, candidates for the next world into citizens of this world, religious and political flunkeys of heavenly monarchs and lords into self-reliant citizens of the earth.[26]

That Promethean humanism which underlies non-realist faith also finds expression in some of Wittgenstein's most rebellious thoughts: 'If I thought of God as another being like myself, outside myself, only infinitely more powerful, then I would regard it as my duty to defy him.'[27] On the other hand, the sense of human self-reliance is more frequently contradicted by the strongest of misanthropies, and a complete disregard for social improvement. Witness the following characteristic anecdote:

> When, in the 'twenties, Russell wanted to establish, or join, a 'World Organization for Peace and Freedom' or something similar, Wittgenstein rebuked him so severely, that Russell said to him: 'Well, I suppose *you* would rather establish a World Organization for War and Slavery', to which Wittgenstein passionately assented: 'Yes, rather that, rather that!'[28]

It was his dark attitude towards human nature which doubtless contributed to the failure of Wittgenstein's Tolstoyan religious experiment.

Whereas Tolstoy could turn to the peasants with love and admiration, Wittgenstein could see only louts and brutes. Possessed of such an outlook, any talk of a humanist religion would surely be dismissed by him as nothing more than crass vapidity.

Moreover, the humanism of the non–realist leads to a tendency to judge and, if necessary, to jettison religious pictures which, for one reason or another, come to be regarded as unhelpful or offensive. Cupitt, for example, speaks of 'modernising Christianity and getting it up to date', a process which involves, among other things, ridding it of any sexist symbolism and ordaining women. What allows such modernisation to occur is the recognition that 'it was we who made our religious beliefs, it is we who are responsible for them, and it is up to us to put them right'.[29] In stark opposition to this stands Wittgenstein's idea that we must not 'pick and choose' when it comes to religion,[30] a theme effectively amplified by Phillips when he claims that such radical theological surgery runs counter to the true spirit of faith. When religious pictures are judged by ethical or political criteria, this results, he says, in

> a curious reversal of the emphasis needed in religion, where the believer does not want to say that he measures these pictures and finds that they are all right or finds that they are wanting. On the contrary, the believers wish to claim that it isn't they who measure the pictures, since in a sense, the pictures measure them; they are the measure in terms of which they judge themselves. They do not judge the picture.[31]

Such sentiments close the door to any revision of Christian faith. If someone feels, say, that the symbolism of religion portrays women in a negative light, or that it is in some manner morally unsound, that person is, according to the Wittgensteinian, in the position of Job, challenging the righteousness of the Lord, and to whom the Lord responded: 'Who is this that darkeneth counsel by words without knowledge? . . . Where wast thou when I laid the foundations of the earth?'[32] It is this conviction that the believer is not to question the ways of God as revealed in the tradition that leads Cupitt ultimately to lament the inherent conservatism of Wittgenstein's religious thinking. It certainly entails that Wittgenstein cannot straightforwardly be counted among the allies of radical theology.

Cupitt has, nevertheless, built upon something he believes to have found in Wittgenstein's work, namely the creative power of the *word*, so that (as Winch puts it) 'the concepts we have settle for us the form of experience we have of the world'.[33] It is undeniably an element of Wittgenstein's thinking that religious discourse makes possible certain experiences, certain views of the world. And Rhees has, for example, highlighted a number of affinities between the language of religion and the language of love which illustrate this fact.[34] A person can only experience love, can only fall in love and be broken up by it, because he has been taught the *language* of love. Of course it would be possible for a person not acquainted with language to be sexually aroused by another. But that would be a matter of biological impulse only. To *experience love* it is necessary to have been schooled in the language of love, a language which makes this particular experience possible. Rhees says the same is true of religion: it is inconceivable that a person could worship God and desire salvation without having been taught the words 'God', 'worship', 'salvation', and their meaning and role within the religious life. And that means, of course, being trained in a particular way, being schooled in religious discourse. Once this vocabulary has been mastered, experiences, attitudes and feelings otherwise closed to a person are opened up.

Though such a view can be discerned in Wittgenstein (in his views, for example, on the Last Judgement and its effects upon the believer), Cupitt presses the idea a good deal harder, maintaining that there is no experience – indeed, no reality – *outside* of language. Such a position we might call 'linguistic idealism'. Cupitt not only advocates it in his own work, but claims furthermore that it is Wittgenstein's own doctrine, so that in his later philosophy we are taught to 'see that language is the creator of everything. In the beginning was the Word.'[35] But, on the contrary, Wittgenstein is less impressed by language's claim to be ultimate creator. For him, as we will now see, it is *action* which receives this appellation: 'Language – I want to say – is a refinement, "in the beginning was the deed"' (CV 31).

5.3 THE NATURAL HISTORY OF RELIGION

Wittgenstein's emphasis on the primacy of deed over deliberation emerges strongly when he considers the nature of pain-language, particularly first-person expressions (*Äusserungen*) of pain (such as 'My leg hurts,' 'I have a toothache,' 'I am in pain'), and the relation of this language to pain-behaviour (groaning, crying, screaming). One held by a Tractarian view of language might be inclined to say that the sentence 'I am in pain' functions as a description of an inner state: I observe that I am experiencing a certain sensation, and identify this sensation as one of pain; I then use language publicly to report to others that I am experiencing this sensation. There are, naturally, occasions on which 'I am in pain' does function as a description (my doctor asks me what the trouble is and I reply, 'I have a pain in my left arm'). Nevertheless, Wittgenstein wants to say that the language of pain does not originate (and does not always or even primarily function) in such a fashion, as a calm description of an inner feeling. Rather:

> Words are connected with the primitive, the natural, expressions of the sensation and used in their place. A child has hurt himself and he cries; and then adults talk to him and teach him exclamations and, later, sentences. They teach the child new pain-behaviour. (PI §244)

Think of what happens as a child matures and learns to control its feelings: instead of crying, the child says 'It hurts.' The word 'pain' is learned, then, not as a description of certain sensations and behaviour, but, rather, as a *replacement* for the non-verbal expression of pain.

Note how pain-language is seen here as a piece of *behaviour*, again illustrating Wittgenstein's wish fully to locate language within activity. The sentence '*He* is in pain' is similarly connected with behaviour, connected with helping, pitying, worrying. And this helping of which the language is a refinement is itself instinctual. We do not (at least as a rule) *infer* from someone's behaviour that that person is in pain ('I groan like that when my body hurts, so she too must be experiencing a similar pain'). No, reason does not come into play on such occasions: 'It is a help here to remember that it is a primitive reaction to tend, to treat, the part that hurts when someone else is in pain; and not merely when oneself is' (Z §540). Wittgenstein continues:

> But what is the word 'primitive' meant to say here? Presumably that this sort of behaviour is *pre-linguistic*: that a language-game is based *on it*, that it is the prototype of a way of thinking and not the result of thought. (Z §541)

The term 'primitive reaction' is introduced to emphasise just how much human behaviour is instinctive and pre-rational in character, and to undermine the rationalistic prejudice that action is always the result of thought. So much of what we do – embracing those we love, comforting those in pain, flinching from danger, brushing an insect off our skin, and so on – is entirely instinctual and with no grounding in thought whatsoever. All of which, of course, coheres with Wittgenstein's stated desire 'to regard man here as an animal; as a primitive being to which one grants instinct but not ratiocination' (OC §475).

To this, one might wish to say, 'This is all very well with regard to matters of pain and tending, for these are largely emotional matters, rather than matters of reason. But what of the more rational elements of human life? Surely Wittgenstein cannot be saying that these are instinctive?' But Wittgenstein *is* saying precisely this. Very sophisticated forms of discourse are, he claims, based upon primitive reactions and are thus related to instinctive action just as the language of pain is related to pre-rational expressive behaviour. Consider the language of causation. One may want to say that the concept of cause and effect stems from the observation of events, so that, for example, I see on a number of occasions stones hitting windows and infer that the breaking of the window is caused by the stone's impact. Wittgenstein's idea of the origination of the concept is far less rationalistic. Indeed, a child is no less adept than a philosopher in employing causal language: 'Calling something "the cause" is like pointing and saying: "*He's* to blame"' (CE 410). Understanding the nature of causality is as immediate as that. He says:

> There is a reaction which can be called 'reacting to the cause'. – We also speak of 'tracing' the cause; a simple case would be, say, following a string to see who is pulling at it. If I then find him – how do I know that he, his pulling, is the cause of the string's moving? Do I establish this by a series of experiments? (CE 416)

The question is patently rhetorical. No such experiments are required, nor is any thinking called for at all. One immediately and instinctively recognises the cause. All subsequent sophisticated discussion of the concept of causation (say, the Aristotelian distinction between material, formal, efficient, and final cause) are elaborations of, and are grafted on to, the basic, animal instinct of 'reacting to the cause'. Without that primitive reaction (were we not the kind of animal inclined to react in such a way), then the later sophisticated talk would have no life and no intelligibility. Moreover, any sceptical doubts concerning causation (such as those famously voiced by Hume) are, for Wittgenstein, secondary to a more fundamental acceptance: 'The primitive form of the language-game is certainty, not uncertainty. For uncertainty could never lead to action' (CE 420).

In the cases we have considered – experience of pain, tending others, tracing a cause – there is no (natural) place for experiment or speculation. We just act; and with certainty, a certainty which has something 'animal' about it. It is only when we are in the grip of rationalistic prejudices that we fail to see how animalistic, how instinctual, are our basic ways of acting and thinking. We think these practices need to be intellectually grounded and justified, but when we observe the behaviour of animals – a spider spinning a web, a cat stalking a mouse – a realisation dawns of the intellectual groundlessness of those actions, and of our own:

> The squirrel does not infer by induction that it is going to need stores next winter as well. And no more do we need a law of induction to justify our actions or our predictions. (OC §287)

Pre-rational action assumes, then, a centre-stage position in Wittgenstein's later thinking. We have already seen that he wants to characterise instinctual, animalistic certainty as a form of life (cf. OC §§358, 359), and in *Zettel* we encounter the striking contention that language is merely 'an extension of primitive behaviour. (For our *language-game* is behaviour.) (Instinct)' (Z §545).

This is such a pronounced aspect of Wittgenstein's later thinking that we should expect it to enter into his reflections on religious belief and practice, and indeed, as hinted earlier, the idea of the primitive reaction does feature prominently in his criticism of Frazer. But moreover, it may well be that this stress on instinctual reactions and shared forms of life provides us with the very key we require to understand Wittgenstein's account of religion, an account which, as we can now see, offers us the outline of a natural history of religion.

The term 'natural history' is, of course, one borrowed from biological science, and, as such, a 'natural history of religion' could be expected to perform analogous tasks. Just as the natural history of a plant might specify how it originates, how it develops, and the conditions in which it thrives and languishes, so too with a natural history of *religion*. Treating religion as some kind of organism, it would be shown how religion develops and what social and psychological conditions must prevail in order for religion to survive. And characteristically, a natural history of religion will attempt to locate the origins of religion, not in some divine revelation to which human beings respond (there we would have *super-natural* history), but in something more mundane. Religion will be seen to have an origin in nature, or, more specifically, in *human* nature.

All these themes are to the fore in Hume's *Natural History of Religion*, in which he attempts to isolate the earliest form of religion. Finding this in polytheism, Hume proceeds to ask how the belief in many gods could have arisen. It is, he says, impossible to imagine that such a system of belief could have arisen from a rational consideration of the world. Rather, it arises out of fear: 'the first ideas of religion arose not from a contemplation of the works of nature, but from a concern with regard to the events of life, and from the incessant hopes and fears, which actuate the human mind'.[36] The motivations underlying the genesis of religion, therefore, were nothing as elevated as the noble desire to serve and worship a sublime deity, for it was instead the desperate hope for happiness and survival, and the anguished fear of misery and death, that filled this role. So much of the natural world – drought, disease, natural disasters – imperiled the existence of our forebears. Ignorant of the true causes of those things which determined their fate, these helpless folk formed primitive notions of great powers lying behind the capricious

phenomena of nature, and, by a natural human tendency to anthropo-
morphism, personified these powers. Thus the gods were born of a most
fearful and vulgar superstition. The emotional origination of religion thus
asserted, Hume illustrates the development of polytheism into monothe-
ism, a transformation which occurs when one favoured deity in the
pantheon is elevated, to the eventual exclusion of all the rest who are
subsequently forgotten. And finally, having isolated fear and ignorance as
the authors of religion, it will be the case that religion will thrive best in
such frightful conditions. By the same token, advancement in both
comfort and knowledge should gnaw at religion's very roots.

It is easy to see how such a natural history might fit into a wider
criticism of religion, for thus to locate the original form of religious belief
will be to demonstrate how it arises from primitive conditions, from the
childhood of the human species. Certainly part of Frazer's motivation in
tracing religion back to its genesis was to provide another weapon for the
atheist's arsenal. Frazer shares much with Hume, principally the conviction that the existence of religion can be attributed in no small part to
human frailty. For Hume this frailty is fear in the face of nature; for
Frazer it is a frailty of intellect, resulting in the primitive's elaboration of a
barren philosophy of life. Both, moreover, trace the development of
religion through history and await eagerly the time when religious
superstition will finally be discarded. In Frazer in particular, this attitude
is tied to a great faith in historical progress and the continuing enlightenment of the human mind by means of science. If enlightenment is the
bedfellow of secularism, then religion must be the darkest sign of
ignorance, standing in the way of happiness and intellectual fulfilment.
It must therefore be rejected.

Stated thus, it may seem queer to suggest that Wittgenstein might
himself be offering something akin to a natural history of religion. Is he
not appalled by Frazer's attack on religion? Does he not oppose those who
view religion as mistaken science? Did he not condemn as 'the stupid
superstition of our time' (RFGB 6) the view that religion arose from
ignorance of the causes of natural phenomena? Indeed he did. And yet
what is perhaps most fruitful in Wittgenstein's thinking on religious
matters are those ideas, nascent in the *Remarks on Frazer* and which can
be supplemented by his talk of primitive reactions, which suggest, just as
much as Hume had earlier done, that the origins and nature of religion
must be attributed to human nature, that its roots lie in humanity's
natural responsiveness to the world.

Wittgenstein's natural history starts by noting some elemental ritual
actions which are the outcome, not of thought, but purely of instinct.
Recall two examples considered earlier: beating a tree when angry, and

kissing a loved one's image. The intellectualist account of such actions –
that they theoretically grounded – is vehemently denied by Wittgenstein.
Such rituals are not founded on opinions,[37] but are instead instances of
what we might choose to call 'pure act': actions performed before any
operation of intellect is brought into play. What experimental reasoning,
what intellectual manoeuvre, did I undertake before kissing my loved
one's picture when my heart bled with want of her? None, obviously. No
thinking enters into the elemental acts of ritual. They hence conform to
the character of the primitive reaction as described in *Zettel*: pre-
linguistic, pre-rational behaviour, which is 'the prototype of thinking
and not the result of thought' (Z §541). These ritual actions are no
aberration, for (as instinctual) they are somehow natural to human beings,
an observation which leads Wittgenstein to describe man as 'a ceremonious animal' (RFGB 7).

Although these ritualistic primitive reactions emerge spontaneously
from human nature, their particular shape arises from human beings'
interaction with their natural environment, conspicuous features of which
Wittgenstein highlights thus:

> That a man's shadow, which looks like a man, or that his mirror image, or that rain,
> thunderstorms, the phases of the moon, the change of seasons, the likenesses and
> differences of animals to one another and to human beings, the phenomena of
> death, of birth and of sexual life, in short everything a man perceives year in, year
> out around him, connected together in any variety of ways – that all this should play
> a part in his thinking (his philosophy) and his practices, is obvious, or in other
> words this is what we really know and find interesting. (RFGB 6)

None of these things are in themselves particularly surprising, for they are
so familiar to us. There is, therefore, no real justification for saying that
primitive man was led to religious belief because he was continually
shocked and stunned by the events of the world, which he tried
(pathetically) to explain. Nevertheless, it is those things which perennially
surround a person that will function as the focus for his ritual expressions.
Two examples will suffice to illustrate this point. In his comments on
Frazer's account of the ancient worship of trees, Wittgenstein highlights,
not the process of reasoning which might have led to the divinisation of
the oak tree, but rather the mode of living which might naturally give rise
to that belief.

> It was not a trivial reason, for really there can have been no *reason*, that prompted
> certain races of mankind to venerate the oak tree, but only the fact that they and the
> oak were united in a community of life, and therefore it was not by choice that they
> arose together, but rather like the flea and the dog. (If fleas developed a rite, it
> would be based on the dog.)[38]

That a religious attitude towards the oak tree could arise will not be a surprise for anyone who has read Frazer's awe-inspiring description of the massive forests dominating the environment of ancient Europe, forests which would profoundly have influenced the life and thought of 'our rude ancestors who dwelt dispersed under the gloomy shadow or in the open glades and clearings of the forest'.[39] For Wittgenstein, it was the sense of dependence on, and life within, the great forests that gave rise to ritual expression in the form of tree worship. In the gloom of the forest the trees would have been the geographical and spiritual parameters of one's life. Nothing could be more natural than that these should have become the focus of the rituals and beliefs of a ceremonious animal.

For a second example, we can note Wittgenstein's response to Drury when the latter related his shock at encountering, in a temple in Egypt, a sexually explicit carving of the god Horus with an erect phallus, ejaculating into a bowl. Wittgenstein is puzzled as to why such a representation should cause alarm and surprise:

> Why in the world shouldn't they have regarded with awe and reverence that act by which the human race is perpetuated? Not every religion has to have St. Augustine's attitude to sex. Why, even in our culture marriages are celebrated in a church; everyone present knows what is going to happen that night, but that doesn't prevent it being a religious ceremony.[40]

Sex is such a prominent aspect of human life that it is perfectly natural for countless rites of passage to be focused upon it (witness the vast preponderance of rituals surrounding puberty, menstruation and wedlock). Along with birth and death, it is the most obvious focus for religious expression, and it is therefore no accident that christenings, marriages and funerals constitute the three most important ritual occasions in a person's life, marking their arrival in the world, their function within it, and their departure from it.

It is not human beings alone, of course, who experience the great trinity of birth, sex and death, nor do we alone interact with our natural environment. The lives of other animals are bounded in the same manner and yet it is only human beings who engage in ritual activity to mark that condition; it is only this ceremonious animal that has such ritualistic instincts, that reacts to images of people, mimics desired events, and so on.[41] We might say, then, that ritual phenomena is a mode of our particular form of life, and that it is, therefore, something typical of human beings, something animal lying beyond justification or critique. Here we can see how the notion of a form of life enters into Wittgenstein's account of religion, though not as a means of characterising a religious person's way of life, nor yet as a way of protecting religion from outside attack. The form of life motif, rather, works alongside the idea of a primitive reaction so as to expose that the roots of religion reside within human nature. To speak of a form of life in this context is to draw attention to those instinctive reactions which are further developed by culture into larger scale religious systems.

To see how this process of development might occur, we can return to the relation of language to pain-behaviour. The initial non-linguistic expression of pain is not the result of any intellectual operation, but is an instinctual primitive reaction. Once language has been grafted on to such expressions, a conceptual space is created within which a fuller articulation, development and indeed experiencing of pain can be effected. Similarly, further development of the primitive reaction of tending another brings about medical care, as well as great creative thought, such as the compassion-rooted moral philosophy of Schopenhauer. And here it is essential to be reminded that without the primitive reaction of tending, no hospitals would have been established, no ethical praise for mercy, for such thoughts and endeavours would be entirely alien to us. Hence Wittgenstein's desire to trace the origin of the language-game to 'a reaction; only from this can more complicated forms develop' (CV 31).

These notions are fully reiterated in Wittgenstein's analysis of religion. As we have seen, the reactions he focuses on are those elemental acts such as the instinctive destruction of an image, and as with the instinctive expression of pain, this primitive behaviour opens up a conceptual space in which a people's desires, fears and views of life can be formulated. That initial reaction, therefore, makes possible the development of a whole view of the world. What is impossible to imagine is that religion might have existed *without* those elemental actions, without that natural rituality. This is a point implicitly present in Wittgenstein's treatment of the doctrine of the Last Judgement. Certainly one is taught from an early age the picture of God judging one's actions at the end of time, and this picture itself gives rise to certain feelings within the believer. But the notion of a Last Judgement could never have come about without some prior feelings of responsibility, guilt and dread. Indeed, that eschatological doctrine is a product of those primitive reactions: 'Why shouldn't one form of life culminate in an utterance of belief in a Last Judgement?' (LC 58). Norman Malcolm's reflections on the ontological argument reach a similar conclusion, when he suggests that the very idea of a merciful God could only have grown out of anterior feelings of guilt and hope for forgiveness. In such a fashion, quite sophisticated religious beliefs are to be understood by tracing them back to natural human feelings and actions, so that a religious system is precisely 'an extension of primitive behaviour' (Z §545), or, as Wittgenstein says in the *Remarks on Frazer*, 'only . . . a later extension of instinct'.[42] Wittgenstein's natural history of religion thus focuses on the development of religion from its roots in instinctive human behaviour, and shows, via the image of man as a ceremonious animal, that this primitive behaviour is definitive of humanity, filling as large a role in the natural history of human beings as does eating, drinking, procreation, playing games, singing, making art, and so on.

To connect religion so intimately with human nature brings with it not just a new perspective on religion. It has also the consequence of throwing light on what it is to be human. This illumination can be disquieting. What happens, for example, when we uncover instances of ritual killing, such as the Aztecs' mass sacrifices of children, or the burning of people during the fire-festivals which formerly occurred throughout Europe? If we think, as Frazer did, that religion is principally an attempt to understand and control the natural world, then we may be able to dismiss the abiding significance of such sacrifices, which may now be seen to belong simply to the errors of our forebears, and to have sprung 'from a mistaken theory of the solar system'.[43] The comfort of such a conclusion is not open to Wittgenstein. If religion springs from human nature, then human beings are that type of strange and sinister creature that burn people alive so as to mark special days. This may well provoke dismay about our natures, and such worries do not disappear simply because human sacrifice is no longer a feature of our culture. The readiness with which a nation may scapegoat a minority community, or even that the killing of animals may be undertaken for sporting pleasure, serves as a constant reminder of the violent propensities dormant within human nature. Now possessed of such unease, we may feel that burning an image of Guy Fawkes on 5 November is less frivolous than it had previously seemed: 'the fact that on certain days children burn a straw man could make us uneasy . . . Strange that they should celebrate by burning a *man*!' (RFGB 18). And even neglecting this undercurrent of violence, religion, as a manifestation of something quintessentially human, reveals to us something queer about the nature of us as a species. What can we make of the fact that we venerate certain images (and destroy others), that we hold certain days more significant than others, that we engage in peculiar rituals? Truly, we are a strange animal. Hence why Wittgenstein's thinking on religion rests ultimately on 'the thought of man and his past, . . . the strangeness of what I see in myself and in others, what I have seen and have heard' (RFGB 18).[44]

5.4 ATHEISM

That Wittgenstein traces the roots of religion to instinctual impulses might lead some to suspect that he is engaged in a critical enterprise, in the same way that Hume's denial of the rational grounding of faith leads him to a view of religion as little more than 'sick men's dreams'.[45] These suspicions may be compounded by the manner in which religion is seen to be a thoroughly human product, an expression of human nature rather than a relationship with transcendent realities: were man not a ceremonious animal, there would be no God. On the other hand, Wittgenstein's unswervingly respectful attitude does not suggest anti-religious frenzy, and if his emphasis on primitive reactions in religious concept-formation denies religion an intellectually respectable foundation, then, as we have seen, he denies the concept of causation such a foundation also, something which does not lead to an abandonment of the language of cause and effect. Similarly, religion is not singled out for attention when conceived as a product of our particular form of life. Mathematics, generally regarded as independent of whatever human beings might think or be capable of, is thoroughly humanised by Wittgenstein, who comes to see it as 'an anthropological phenomenon' (RFM 180): we could not engage in geometry were we, like other animals, unable to distinguish a triangle from a rectangle, while the mathematical use of negation is simply 'an ethnological fact – it's something to do with the way we live' (LFM 249). In this respect, then, Wittgenstein's later account of religion differs little in character from his treatment of all other concepts and activities, none of which emerge from reasoning (cf. OC §475) and all of which are products of the manner in which humans live, and the capabilities we possess.

It would, none the less, be somewhat perplexing were someone to accept all that Wittgenstein has to say about religion in his later period and yet still be able to continue in his or her faith, or that a person might be converted to Christianity having understood it in Wittgenstein's terms.[46] Once, that is, one had come to a recognition that Christianity is a set of admonishing pictures tied into a particular way of living, and once the fountainhead of religion is located in an instinctive way of reacting to the world, could one's faith in God feasibly remain intact? In other words, though Wittgenstein's attention to the depth grammar of religious discourse may well have revealed its true nature, does not a person's own belief depend for its continued life on an acceptance of the surface grammar of religion? Do not believers have to think that there is a God, that there will be an afterlife, that there have been miraculous occurrences, and so on, in order to engage in the religious life? As John Searle has remarked, 'You have to be a very *recherché* sort of religious intellectual to keep praying if you don't think there is any real God outside the language who is listening to your prayers.'[47] Our question now then is whether atheism is the inevitable consequence of an acceptance of Wittgenstein's approach to religious belief, and what kind of atheism this could be.

This matter can profitably be addressed by considering the character of Wittgenstein's personal religious position. We have already had cause to explore those passages from *Culture and Value* illustrating his inclination towards belief. Yet this inclination is of a somewhat idiosyncratic order, and appears to arise from traits of Wittgenstein's own distinctive character, rather than either bespeaking wholehearted commitment or describing a faith which others might plausibly decide to embrace. Hence, from Norman Malcolm's *Memoir*:

> Wittgenstein did once say that he thought that he could understand the conception of God, in so far as it is involved in one's awareness of one's own sin and guilt. He added that he could *not* understand the conception of a *Creator*. I think that the ideas of Divine judgement, forgiveness, and redemption had some intelligibility for him, as being related in his mind to feelings of disgust with himself, an intense desire for purity, and a sense of the helplessness of human beings to make themselves better. But the notion of a being *making the world* had no intelligibility for him at all.[48]

Similarly, Wittgenstein feels unable to call Jesus 'Lord', '*Because I do not believe* that he will come to judge me; because *that* says nothing to me' (CV 33). And then we have what is perhaps the most significant of his expressions of unbelief:

> I am not a religious man but I cannot help seeing every problem from a religious point of view.[49]

This comment encapsulates two determining features of Wittgenstein's approach to religious belief: first, the extent to which he was drawn with awe towards the religious view of the world; and second, his own inability fully to share in that perspective.

But why did he feel unable to believe? One possibility is perhaps contained in Wittgenstein's reflections on why he could not pray: 'I cannot kneel to pray because it's as though my knees were stiff. I am afraid of dissolution (of my own dissolution), should I become soft' (CV 56). To Malcolm, this suggests that Wittgenstein's lack of faith may have arisen from the completeness with which he engaged in the philosophical task, an engagement which he feared would be fatally disturbed were he to turn to the prayerful life of faith.[50] While that is an interesting thought, it does not fully convince, for Wittgenstein made many attempts precisely to extricate himself from the philosophical work which so tormented his mind. It seems therefore unlikely that it would have been a desire to continue with that work which would have resulted in his denial of faith. On the contrary, the religious life might have offered the perfect way out. Consider now a very different possibility, arising from yet another of Drury's recollections:

> We called round at my brother's architectural office in Bedford Circus . . . One of the assistant draughtsmen was designing an altar cross. Wittgenstein became quite agitated: 'I couldn't for the life of me design a cross in this age; I would rather go to hell than try and design a cross.'[51]

It may well be, then, that it was something about the character of 'this age' which constrained his religious impulses. Further attention to this may confirm our earlier suggestion that, far from Wittgenstein being the fideistic friend of religion hoped for by apologists and derided by Nielsen, the consequence of his later thought on religion is an unavoidable acceptance of atheism. In order to see why this is the case we need to focus upon two issues: Wittgenstein's view of religion as a product of human culture; and his pessimistic analysis of 'this age'.

We have already seen how Wittgenstein considers religion to have its roots in human nature, but he also sees it crucially as giving expression to, and glorifying, the values lying at the heart of a particular culture. This is a point well made in the *Remarks on Frazer*. Frazer has described the nature of a kingship in which a candidate for the title must kill the incumbent and will himself eventually be killed. Rather than uncovering the motives and beliefs which might have led to such a rule of succession, Wittgenstein stresses instead that this practice manifests a principle dear to that culture, that principle being 'the majesty of death' (RFGB 3). A nation of cowards could never hold such a value, and thus no such rule of succession would decide its kingship. Similarly, if a culture's members ceased to have any sense of responsibility for wrongdoing, the idea of a final judgement could never enter into their religious beliefs. The fate of religious belief is not unaffected, then, by the changes a culture might undergo; and if a culture dies, then its gods die with it. The position of religion is hence precarious, being at the mercy of the twists and turns of history and culture.

It is precisely here that Wittgenstein's stark cultural pessimism makes its uncomfortable presence felt on the very possibility of religious belief. To see why this should be so, we need to pay a little attention to the thought of one of the greatest influences on Wittgenstein's philosophy: Oswald Spengler. In *The Decline of the West*, Spengler offers a vision of history diametrically at odds with those progressive accounts (such as that offered by Hegel) which optimistically detect in history a movement away from ignorance and barbarism and towards ever-improving societal arrangement and intellectual achievement. Rejecting that view of one linear history, Spengler saw instead:

the drama of a *number* of mighty Cultures, each springing with primitive strength
from the soil of a mother-region to which it remains firmly bound throughout its
whole life-cycle; each stamping its material, its mankind, in *its own* image; each
having *its own* idea, *its own* passions, *its own* life, will and feeling, *its own* death . . .
Each Culture has its own new possibilities of self-expression which arise, ripen,
decay, and never return.[52]

A culture is here envisaged as an organism, and it can be analysed in an
analogous fashion to the way the life-cycle of a plant can be described. If
we observe the life of a flower, we see it first as a little shoot springing
from its mother-soil; its bud appears, and it then blossoms before
withering away into death. Likewise, says Spengler, a culture emerges
energetically, and brings forth great art, music, poetry, metaphysical
systems, *and its own religion*, before all possibilities of artistic creation
disappear as it wilts, as our Western culture has, into materialism and
triviality. Although religion is a mark of the vibrancy of a culture, it has
for Spengler no life independent of it, and hence its destiny is to die. The
possibility of belief is no longer open in an age such as ours, not even to
those who mourn its passing. They must accept that the possibility for
belief has vanished, for to do otherwise would be akin to the dying flower
longing to bloom again:

The megalopolitan *is* irreligious; this is part of his being, a mark of his historical
position. Bitterly as he may feel the inner emptiness and poverty, earnestly as he
may long to be religious, it is out of his power to be so. All religiousness in the
Megalopolis rests upon self-deception.[53]

The lesson from Spengler is that the possibility of religious belief is
determined by what is allowed and what is disallowed by a culture's stage
of development. And given that we are living 'a *late* life',[54] given that our
culture is in a state of decline, we have no option but to accept atheism.
    Wittgenstein made no secret of his own indebtedness to Spengler
(cf. CV 19), and it is remarkable just how much his thought is permeated
with the motif of *decline*. In his preface to the *Investigations*, for example, he
speaks of 'the darkness of this time' (PI p. viii); he considered the notion of
scientific progress 'a delusion' and 'a trap' (CV 56); and a comparison
between the great figures of our time (Russell, Freud and Einstein) and
those of a previous era (Beethoven, Schubert and Chopin) led him
distressedly to bewail 'the terrible degeneration that had come over the
human spirit in the course of only a hundred years'.[55] More significantly
for our purposes, however, Wittgenstein's perception of this decline led
him to a re-evaluation of the philosophical enterprise. When he returned to
Cambridge in 1929, Wittgenstein spent much time considering what the

proper role of philosophy should be, eventually arriving at the idea of a therapeutic technique aimed at removing confused metaphysical problems. Concerning this transformation of philosophy from a quasi-mystical and perhaps visionary subject into a method, he says:

> The nimbus of philosophy has been lost. For we now have a method of doing philosophy, and can speak of *skilful* philosophers . . . But once a method has been found the opportunities for the expression of personality are correspondingly restricted. The tendency of our age is to restrict such opportunities; this is characteristic of an age of declining culture or without culture. (WLL 21)

One is struck by the extent to which Wittgenstein's philosophical project meets the restrictions laid down by Spengler concerning what is and is not possible in an age of decline. Visionary metaphysics, art, poetry, are all debarred and technics elevated in their place.[56] Wittgenstein's transformation of philosophy into a method for destroying metaphysics seems, then, to have been enacted on Spenglerian advice. And if Wittgenstein's view of the nature of philosophy was dictated by his reading of Spengler, then it is not unlikely that he would have been of the opinion that religion too is at the mercy of culture's decline, and that faith was no longer a living option in 'the darkness of this time', a time in which science dominates and sends our wondering spirit to sleep (cf. CV 5).

The conclusions thus reached can only be unsettling for believers. We have already seen that it would be hard for Wittgenstein's later account of religion to be embraced by the faithful, and yet it is this historical undercurrent of his thinking, this intuition that religion is not possible in our time, which gives his account a distinctly atheistic character. This is not an atheism based on denying the existence of super-empirical realities (religion never was about that), nor is it the rebellious atheism of an Ivan Karamazov, nor yet is it the positivistic atheism of denying sense to religious propositions. It is, rather, a despairing, apocalyptic atheism that arises from Wittgenstein's philosophy of religion, the frustrated and bitter recognition that the passionate beauty of the religious life is no longer open to us. We are, of course, still ceremonious animals, so may continue to mark occasions with strange festivities and with ceremony, and yet the possibility of living one's life in relationship with God must be surrendered. And as stoic resignation has been seen to be definitive of faith, this final renunciation may itself be regarded as an act of the deepest piety.

NOTES

1. Wittgenstein, quoted in M. O'C. Drury, 'Some Notes on Conversations with Wittgenstein', in Rhees (ed.), *Recollections of Wittgenstein* (Oxford: Oxford University Press, 1984), p. 90.

2. Wittgenstein, in ibid., p. 86.

3. See J. L. Mackie, *The Miracle of Theism* (Oxford: Clarendon Press, 1982), especially pp. 251–3.

4. Richard Swinburne, *The Existence of God* (Oxford: Clarendon Press, 1979), p. 291.

5. Wittgenstein, quoted in Drury, 'Some Notes on Conversations with Wittgenstein', p. 90.

6. D. Z. Phillips, *Faith after Foundationalism* (London: Routledge, 1988), p. 10.

7. Basil Mitchell, *The Justification of Religious Belief* (London: Macmillan, 1973), p. 99.

8. Ibid., p. 117.

9. Ibid., p. 118.

10. Wittgenstein, quoted in Drury, 'Some Notes on Conversations with Wittgenstein', p. 86.

11. Leo Tolstoy, *A Confession and Other Religious Writings* (Harmondsworth: Penguin, 1987), p. 87.

12. Ibid., p. 35.

13. Ibid., p. 58.

14. Ibid., p. 59.

15. Ibid., p. 63.

16. On Tolstoy's treatment of the acceptance of death, see his story *The Death of Ivan Ilyich* (Harmondsworth: Penguin, 1960).

17. Wittgenstein, quoted in Drury, 'Conversations with Wittgenstein', in Rhees (ed.), *Recollections of Wittgenstein* (Oxford: Oxford University Press, 1984), p. 114.

18. Paul Engelmann, *Letters from Ludwig Wittgenstein* (Oxford: Basil Blackwell, 1967), p. 41 (letter dated 2 January 1921).

19. Leo Tolstoy, *Twenty-three Tales* (Oxford: Oxford University Press, 1906), p. 181.

20. Friedrich Nietzsche, *The Will to Power* (New York: Vintage, 1968), pp. 124–5.

21. Anthony Freeman, *God in Us* (London: SCM Press, 1993), p. 24.

22. Don Cupitt, *The Sea of Faith* (London: BBC Books, 1984), p. 225.

23. D. Z. Phillips, *Religion Without Explanation* (Oxford: Basil Blackwell, 1976), p. 148.

24. Don Cupitt, *Taking Leave of God* (London: SCM Press, 1980), p. 8.

25. Ibid., p. 116.

26. Ludwig Feuerbach, *Lectures on the Essence of Religion* (New York: Harper & Row, 1967), p. 23.

27. Wittgenstein, quoted in Drury, 'Conversations with Wittgenstein', p. 108.

28. Paul Engelmann, quoted in Ray Monk, *Ludwig Wittgenstein* (London: Vintage, 1991), p. 211.

29. Don Cupitt, 'Anti-Realist Faith', in J. Runzo (ed.), *Is God Real?* (London: Macmillan, 1993), p. 54.

30. See Rush Rhees, 'Picking and Choosing', in D. Z. Phillips (ed.), *Rush Rhees on Religion and Philosophy* (Cambridge: Cambridge University Press, 1997), pp. 307–17.

31. D. Z. Phillips, *Faith and Philosophical Enquiry* (London: Routledge & Kegan Paul, 1970), pp. 117–18.

32. Job 38:2,4 (King James Version).

33. Peter Winch, *The Idea of a Social Science* (London: Routledge & Kegan Paul, 1958), p. 15. Note also Wittgenstein in the *Tractatus*: 'the limits of *language* . . . mean the limits of *my* world' (TLP 5.62).

34. See Rush Rhees, 'Religion and Language', in *Rush Rhees on Religion and Philosophy*, pp. 39–49.

35. Cupitt, *The Sea of Faith*, p. 220.

36. David Hume, *The Natural History of Religion* (Oxford: Oxford University Press, 1993), p. 139.

37. 'The characteristic feature of primitive man, I believe, is that he does not act from *opinions* he holds about things' (RFGB 12).

38. Wittgenstein, 'Remarks on Frazer's *Golden Bough*', in C. G. Luckhardt (ed.), *Wittgenstein: Sources and Perspectives* (Hassocks: The Harvester Press, 1979), pp. 72–3.

39. J. G. Frazer, *The Magic Art and the Evolution of Kings*, (London: Macmillan, 1911), vol. II, p. 350.

40. Wittgenstein, quoted in Drury, 'Conversations with Wittgenstein', p. 148.

41. Some might choose to take issue with this, detecting hints of ritual in the behaviour of non-human animals (see Konrad Lorenz, *On Aggression* (London: Methuen, 1967), pp. 47–71). Such a discovery would not undermine Wittgenstein's thoughts, however, and would in fact serve only to bolster his idea of ritual as a primitive reaction originating in instinct.

42. Wittgenstein, 'Remarks on Frazer's *Golden Bough*', p. 80.

43. Frazer, *The Magic Art and the Evolution of Kings*, vol. I, p. 315.

44. There is insufficient space here for a full consideration of Wittgenstein's fascinating thoughts on human sacrifice as these emerge in his treatment of the Beltane festival, but see *Remarks on Frazer's Golden Bough*, pp. 13–18; Frank Cioffi, 'Wittgenstein and the Fire-Festivals', in *Wittgenstein on Freud and Frazer* (Cambridge: Cambridge University Press, 1998), pp. 80–106; Brian R. Clack, *Wittgenstein, Frazer and Religion* (London: Macmillan, 1999), pp. 135–54.

45. Hume, *The Natural History of Religion*, p. 184.

46. Wittgenstein's earlier account seems to me perfectly compatible with religious belief, for it suggests that lying beyond the mundane world is something 'higher', something ineffable, and that account therefore shares much with classic mysticism as defined by William James (see *The Varieties of Religious Experience* (London: Fontana, 1960), pp. 367–8).

47. John Searle, conversation with Bryan Magee in the latter's *The Great Philosophers* (London: BBC Books, 1987), p. 345.

48. Norman Malcolm, *Ludwig Wittgenstein: A Memoir* (Oxford: Oxford University Press, 1984), p. 59.

49. Wittgenstein, quoted in Drury, 'Some Notes on Conversations with Wittgenstein', p. 79.

50. See Norman Malcolm, *Wittgenstein: A Religious Point of View?* (London: Routledge, 1993), p. 22.

51. Drury, 'Conversations with Wittgenstein', p. 134.

52. Oswald Spengler, *The Decline of the West* (London: George Allen & Unwin, 1926), p. 21.

53. Ibid., pp. 409–10.

54. Ibid., p. 40.

55. Wittgenstein, quoted in Drury, 'Conversations with Wittgenstein', p. 112.

56. See Spengler, *The Decline of the West*, p. 41.

FURTHER READING

Because it is rewarding to study Wittgenstein's philosophy in connection with the events of his extraordinary life, it is worth starting with a biography. Ray Monk's *Ludwig Wittgenstein: The Duty of Genius* (Jonathan Cape, 1990) is a superb account, as is *Wittgenstein: A Life* by Brian McGuinness (Duckworth, 1988). Moving memoirs and recollections of Wittgenstein include Paul Engelmann's *Letters from Ludwig Wittgenstein with a Memoir* (Basil Blackwell, 1967) and Norman Malcolm's *Ludwig Wittgenstein: A Memoir* (Oxford University Press, 1984), while the Rush Rhees-edited *Recollections of Wittgenstein* includes Drury's remarkable records of conversations, and much else besides. *Wittgenstein's Vienna* by Allan Janik and Stephen Toulmin (Weidenfeld & Nicolson, 1973) provides both invaluable insights into the cultural influences on Wittgenstein's thinking and a thought-provoking account of the aims of the *Tractatus*. For those interested in Wittgenstein's non-philosophical work, the beautifully illustrated *Ludwig Wittgenstein: Architect* by Paul Wijdeveld (Thames & Hudson, 1994) is a brilliant account of Wittgenstein's architectural project, while William Warren Bartley's (somewhat notorious) *Wittgenstein* (Quartet, 1977) examines Wittgenstein's life during the 1920s.

For good introductions to Wittgenstein's philosophical work, use A. J. Ayer's *Ludwig Wittgenstein* (Penguin, 1986), *Wittgenstein's Conception of Philosophy* by K. T. Fann (Basil Blackwell, 1969), or A. C. Grayling's *Wittgenstein* (Oxford University Press, 1988). More advanced studies are provided by P. M. S. Hacker in his revised edition of *Insight and Illusion* (Clarendon Press, 1986) and by Norman Malcolm in the excellent *Wittgenstein: Nothing is Hidden* (Basil Blackwell, 1986). Working through Wittgenstein's major works can be assisted by using a good commentary. The *Tractatus Logico-Philosophicus* is a daunting read, which can be made a little easier by the use of such guides as *An Introduction to Wittgenstein's Tractatus* by G. E. M. Anscombe (Hutchinson, 1959), *Wittgenstein's Tractatus: An Introduction* by H. O. Mounce (Basil Blackwell, 1981), and

Wittgenstein's Early Philosophy by Donald Peterson (University of Toronto Press, 1990). Similarly, a reading of the *Philosophical Investigations* can be greatly illuminated by Garth Hallet's *A Companion to Wittgenstein's Philosophical Investigations* (Cornell University Press, 1977), while the multi-volume *Analytical Commentary on Wittgenstein's Philosophical Investigations* by G. P. Baker and P. M. S. Hacker (Basil Blackwell) pays meticulous attention to each of Wittgenstein's paragraphs while also containing excellent clarificatory essays.

On Wittgenstein's philosophy of religion, the definitive work is Cyril Barrett's *Wittgenstein on Ethics and Religious Belief* (Blackwell, 1991). Other important studies include: Alan Keightley's *Wittgenstein, Grammar and God* (Epworth, 1976); *Theology after Wittgenstein* by Fergus Kerr (Basil Blackwell, 1986); *Wittgenstein and Religious Belief* by W. Donald Hudson (Macmillan, 1975); *Logic and Sin in the Writings of Ludwig Wittgenstein* by Philip R. Shields (University of Chicago Press, 1993); while my own *Wittgenstein, Frazer and Religion* (Macmillan, 1999) explores Wittgenstein's thinking on magic and primitive religion. For the work of neo-Wittgensteinians, see D. Z. Phillips' many books, especially *The Concept of Prayer* (Routledge & Kegan Paul, 1965), *Death and Immortality* (Macmillan, 1970), *Religion without Explanation* (Basil Blackwell, 1976), *Faith after Foundationalism* (Routledge, 1988), and *Wittgenstein and Religion* (Macmillan, 1993). See also the essays on religion in Peter Winch's *Trying to Make Sense* (Basil Blackwell, 1987), and those of Rush Rhees in *Rush Rhees on Religion and Philosophy* (edited by D. Z. Phillips, Cambridge University Press, 1997).

INDEX

CPSIA information can be obtained
at www.ICGtesting.com
Printed in the USA
'SHW010948310722
_8742JS00005B/148